THE SEA COMET

By:
Mustafa A. Nejem

The Sea Comet
Copyright © 2023 by Mustafa A. Nejem

All rights reserved.

"There is something in the salt sea air that is very captivating."

- Ernest Hemingway

Table of Contents

Chapter 01

A STRANGE GLOW
A NORMAL DAY

Sarah woke with the sunrise as she always did. Living alone by the coast, she had grown used to solitary mornings listening to the waves and calls of seabirds waking up outside her window. After making a simple breakfast, she got dressed in her worn fishing gear—waterproof trousers and jacket, boots, and hat.

Grabbing her rod and bait box, she headed down to the rocky shore. The tide was out, leaving pools between the boulders that would be teeming with crabs and small fish worth checking. As Sarah peered into the first pool, she heard footsteps crunching on shells behind her.

"Morning Thomas," she called without looking back. Only one person other than herself walked this beach.

"Mornin' Sarah. Catch anything good yet?" responded the deep voice of the elderly fisherman.

"Just getting started. How's your net traps doing?" Sarah asked as Thomas came to stand beside the pool, leaning on his cane.

"Couple good-sized cod in the traps overnight. Reckon the fishing will be fair today if this swell don't pick up too much," Thomas replied gazing out to sea.

Sarah began gently lifting rocks to see what creatures scuttled out from the shadows below. A few shore crabs scurried away while a scolding gull swooped down hoping for an easy meal. After checking a few more likely spots, she turned up an interesting pool holding a swarm of tiny silver fish no longer than her little finger.

"Haven't seen these fellows down here before," Sarah commented to Thomas, holding one of the wriggling fish in her cupped hands. Its sides flashed in iridescent blues and greens as it flailed.

Thomas peered closely at the unusual find through his thick-lensed glasses. "Now that is a rare sight. Those be juvenile moonfish if I ain't mistaken. Don't venture inshore often, must've been washed down in the last high tide..."

Their conversation was cut short by a tremor passing through the rocks and waves that momentarily stole their balance. Both steadied themselves and glanced around curiously for the source. The sea seemed unchanged but a strange smell lingered in the air - metallic and acrid like a storm was brewing yet the sky remained clear.

"Now what in blazes was that about?" Thomas muttered with a frown. Sarah could only shake her head, equally puzzled.

Sarah released the tiny fish back into its rock pool home. Another tremor rumbled through the shore, stronger than before.

"We best get off these rocks, something doesn't feel right," said Thomas as he scanned the horizon. Sarah nodded in agreement and followed him up the beach.

A flash in the distant sky caught their attention. "Look there!" called Sarah, shielding her eyes from the morning sun. A bright trail was cutting across the clouds, glowing orange and burning intensely. But it moved with strange sideways motion unlike any meteor.

Before them, the sea suddenly erupted in a thunderous crack as if struck by lightning. A towering plume of water rose up accompanied by an earsplitting boom. Sarah lost her balance and fell, heart pounding. When she regained her footing, the eerie sight greeted her eyes.

Where the bright flash had disappeared into the ocean, an orange glow emanated beneath the waves. She turned to Thomas who stood transfixed, fear and wonder battling on his wrinkled face.

"All my years and never seen the likes of that," he finally said in a hoarse whisper. The strange glow pulsed in the choppy water as if something below was disturbed yet calming. Sarah began to dread whatever turmoil this omen portended for the sea she had known all her life so well.

A raspy squawk sounded above them. Looking up, they saw gulls circling uncomfortably with distressed cries that were carried off by the persistent offshore breeze. What mysterious force had touched down in their waters this day, and what changes might it bring? For now, only the eerie glow remained as a sign of unseen disturbance in the deep.

Sarah and Thomas stood watching the pulsating glow for several long moments, unsure of what to make of this bizarre event.

"We ought to get you home, lass," Thomas finally said, putting a gentle hand on Sarah's shoulder. She nodded numbly in response. Whatever had happened out there, standing around gawking wouldn't provide any answers.

As they made their way back up the beach, Sarah's mind raced. What could have caused such an explosion? She had never heard of a meteor striking the sea with such force. And the strange glowing aftermath was unlike anything natural.

When they reached her small house, Sarah turned to Thomas. "Please let me know if anything else unsettling occurs. And be careful out there - who knows what effect this may have."

The old fisherman nodded solemnly. "Aye, you can count on it. Best get your thoughts in order too. Mark my words, this will mean change for our shores, though what kind remains unseen."

He gave her a tip of his cap before slowly making his way home, leaning heavily on his cane. Sarah stood watching until his stooped figure disappeared around the rocky headland.

The memory of the massive water column and ethereal glow replayed in her mind. She went inside, but rest would not come. Instead, she fetched her notebook and set to recording every detail of the astounding event, hoping someday to solve the mystery of what had truly fallen from the sky into their peaceful ocean world.

That evening, as the sun sank below the horizon, Sarah returned to the shore. The strange glow was gone, but an uneasiness lingered over the sea. She sat gazing out at the darkening waters, lost in thought.

A splash in the surf nearby startled her from her reverie. Shining her flashlight out, she spotted a large fish struggling in the shallows. Its silvery form seemed to pulsate with an inner light. As Sarah watched, transfixed, the fish gave one last effort and flung itself back into the waves, its glowing shape flickering briefly below the surface before disappearing into the depths.

She shivered, though not from the chill sea breeze. What power now stirred beneath those familiar tides? Only time would reveal the changes wrought by the comet's impact. For now, all was dim and peaceful on the reflective coastline. But Sarah felt in her core that nothing would be the same. She tucked her notebook under one arm and began the walk up the cliff path beneath a sky thick with stars, each one a reminder that forces beyond her control guided the ocean's mysterious currents of change.

Back in her cozy home, Sarah brewed herself a hot drink and settled by the window with pen in hand. Under the stars' wan light, she continued capturing observations of the day's uncanny events, wondering what new marvels or mysteries tomorrow's tide might bring rolling in.

A Bright Streak in the Sky

The next morning, Sarah awoke before dawn as usual. But instead of her morning routine, her thoughts kept drifting back to the previous day's astounding events. Giving up on more sleep, she rose to watch the first hints of sunrise touching the sea.

As color slowly bled into the eastern sky, movement caught her eye. Stepping outside, Sarah scanned the horizon and saw a familiar figure making his way down the beach. She grabbed her jacket and greeted Thomas.

"Good morning. Any sign of...anything?" she asked anxiously. Thomas shook his head.

"All's quiet as the tide. Though the fish weren't biting much this dawn. Come, let me show ye something."

Sarah followed him a short way up the beach. Kneeling, Thomas pointed to an area of wet sand dotted with tide pools. At first she saw only ripples and pebbles. Then her eyes adjusted to a crowd of tiny silver fish clustering in the shallows.

"Moonfish!" exclaimed Sarah. "But why are they here?"

Thomas shrugged. "Beats me, lass. Maybe they were spooked by yesterday too. The water's full of 'em all along the shore now."

Sarah crouched to observe the delicate fish, no longer than her fingernail. Their minute forms darted and flickered, reflecting the sunrise in flecks of turquoise and rose-gold.

"They're beautiful. I hope whatever scared them didn't do harm," she said softly. But an ominous feeling lingered that all was not right in their coastal haven.

A sudden bright flash overhead jolted Sarah to her feet with a gasp. She spun to see a streak of brilliant light arcing across the pink-tinged sky. It moved swiftly at first before beginning to slow, its fiery glow bathing the clouds below in hues of neon orange.

"Another one!" breathed Thomas in awe.

They watched transfixed as the glowing object changed course erratically, skipping across the stratosphere like a pebble on water. Its speed decreased further until it seemed to hover motionless, suspended in the upper air.

A deep rumble shook the beach, rising rapidly in intensity. The brilliant dot flared blindingly, then plunged earthward trailing blazing tendrils behind it.

"It's coming down near the cliffs!" shouted Sarah, pointing eagerly.

The hurtling light grew until it filled half the sky, thrashing violently from side to side. Another deafening boom rolled across the sea as it struck somewhere out of view beyond the rocky promontory.

Sarah and Thomas stayed frozen, straining fruitlessly to see through the headland. Then without warning, a massive geyser erupted on the horizon with a sound like the end of the world. A shockwave buffeted them fiercely as a column of steam and spray towered into the pale blue vault of dawn.

As the plume began to rain back to earth, Sarah turned to Thomas. His face was ashen, eyes wide with fear and wonderment behind his glasses.

"Whatever in God's name was that?" she breathed.

"I've no answer for ye, lass," Thomas replied shakily. "But mark my words - this bodes ill for our shores."

Sarah gazed back at the place where something fiery had just met the sea with horrific force. Billowing mist still obscured the impact site. An acrid smell assaulted her senses, like hot metal meeting cold water.

"We must see what manner of beast has visited this wrath upon our coast," she declared, already striding purposefully down the beach. Thomas hesitated.

"Sarah, 'tis not safe. Best we wait and watch from a distance." But his pleas fell on deaf ears.

When they reached the foot of the towering sea cliffs, Sarah began scrambling up the treacherous slope without a backwards glance. Thomas cursed under his breath and gingerly followed.

After much huffing and scrambling over loose shale and jagged rocks, they hauled themselves over the precipice at the top. What lay before them took Sarah's breath away.

Where towering breakers had crashed against the cliffs just that morning, now a jagged scar rent the shoreline. Smoking debris littered the beach and churned in the surf. But most terrible was the churning deep where something still heaved and pulsated, throwing up ominous bubbles tinged fluorescent orange.

As Sarah and Thomas peered down in stunned horror, the pulsing mass beneath the waves gave one final convulsion. A deafening crack split the air, and a colossal fountain erupted skyward accompanied by an unearthly shriek that sent flocks of terrified seabirds wheeling away.

When the waters collapsed back into the boiling froth, two glowing orbs the size of wagon wheels broke the surface, spinning madly. Rearing upward on a nightmarish skeletal frame was a huge, misshapen beast the color of poison. It uttered another inhuman scream that seemed to rip at the fabric of the world.

Sarah's hands flew to her mouth to stifle a sob of terror and dismay. Beside her, even gruff old Thomas appeared ready to faint dead away.

The monster thrashed violently for several moments before collapsing back beneath the waves, its fading cries drifting eerily across the tide-swept rocks. An acrid smoke rose from the churning waters, stinging their eyes.

When at last it seemed the creature had sank for good, a profound silence fell. The only sounds were the wind sighing through sea-grass and the muffled gurgle of surf. Sarah turned slowly to Thomas, who merely shook his stricken face and whispered:

"May God have mercy...what curse have we witnessed being born this day?"

Sarah could not tear her eyes away from the disturbed waters where the monster had appeared. A thousand questions swirled in her mind but no answers emerged.

Thomas placed a trembling hand on her shoulder. "Come away now, lass. We've seen more than enough."

She nodded mutely and followed him back down the treacherous cliff path. When they reached the beach, Sarah collapsed onto a weathered log, head in hands. Thomas sat heavily beside her.

For a long while neither spoke. Offshore, strange cries and splashes drifted to their ears, as if the sea itself was unsettled.

Finally Sarah broke the silence. "What came down from the sky, Thomas? And what new evils now stir in our waters?"

The old fisherman shook his head gravely. "I've no answers, child. But whatever fate or force has touched our shores, I fear 'twill change all."

He sighed wearily, gazing out at the place where ominous ripples still disturbed the waves. "Mark my words - our oceans will ne'er be the same."

Sarah shuddered, drawing her coat tighter. Darkness was falling, yet in her heart a deeper shadow had been cast over the familiar coast and all who lived along its tideline. Only Time would tell what strangeness the morrow's tide might bring rolling in.

Trouble in the Tide Pools

That night, Sarah could barely sleep for visions of glowing eyes and twisting forms boiling up from the depths. When dawn broke, she rose stiff and unrested to scour the beach for clues to the prior day's mysteries.

The cliff where the monster had emerged appeared unchanged, waves lapping innocently at its base. Yet an oily sheen discolored patches of foam that drifted ashore, carrying a putrid smell.

Further exploring, Sarah came upon Thomas examining a tide pool choked with deceased fish and crabs. Their shells were oddly discolored and bodies bloated.

"A grim sight," she said somberly. Thomas nodded grimly.

"Ay, and there's been others like this up and down the cove since dawn. Something fouled the water, that's certain."

He scooped a dead crab from the scum-coated pool, holding it up for inspection. Angry red boils had erupted across its shell and limbs.

"Some foul plague seems to have took hold here," Thomas continued darkly. "And I've no notion what devilry caused it."

As they spoke, shrieks and splashes arose from farther down the strand. Exchanging worried looks, Sarah and Thomas picked their way hastily along the tideline.

Rounding a rocky spur, they beheld a grisly scene: dozens of distressed seabirds flapped and dived wildly around the churning surf. More cries sounded from within crashing waves flecked with crimson foam.

Sarah and Thomas hastened closer in alarm. Between the breakers they glimpsed struggling shapes – not birds but fish, multitudes of them writhing in the surf.

"God above," Thomas breathed. "What ails the poor creatures?"

The fish thrashed in agony, many with raw wounds or milky film clouding their eyes. Gulls swooped to snatch easy prey while others lay still on the wet sand, already passed.

A foreboding sense crept over Sarah. "This is no natural happening. Come, we must—"

A piercing shriek rang out, cutting her off. They spun to see a seagull crash down among the tide pools, convulsing madly as foam frothed around its beak. Before their eyes, grisly boils erupted across its white feathers. Within moments it stiffened and went still.

Thomas took a fearful step back. "Witchcraft...or worse."

As if summoned, a frightful wail arose from far off shore, followed by splashes that caused even the seabirds to flee squawking inland.

Sarah grabbed Thomas' arm. "We must away from here. Now!"

He needed no urging, leaning heavily on his cane as they hastened up the beach. Sarah spared one last glance back – and froze in horror. On the rocky bar between the coves, a shining orange form heaved itself from the tide.

Sarah gasped and pulled Thomas behind a large boulder. Peering around the edge, they watched in terrified wonder.

Before them on the barrens stood an immense creature the color of flames, its gleaming carapace chitinous and misshapen. Where limbs should be, instead writhed twisting tendrils that plunged into the surf, stirring the waters to an unearthly glow.

Its body pulsated and roiled as if some mass within strained for escape. When at last a gaping wound tore open with a sickening squelch, from the bloody cavity emerged two smaller beasts—larva or offspring, whatever their kind.

The monsters scrabbled and writhed on stubby legs, twisting frantically toward the sea. A keening wail escaped their mother as her body visibly shrank.

At last the brooding creature collapsed and went still. The young paused to let out vibrations that made Sarah's teeth ache. As one, they hurled themselves into the roiling surf and were gone.

Once more an eerie silence fell. Sarah slumped against the boulder, strength drained from watching the unnatural birth. Thomas stood stone-faced, hand clasped to his breast as if to calm his pounding heart.

"May all the saints preserve us," he whispered at last. "There can be no doubt - these shores have become accursed."

Sarah couldn't take her eyes off the barrens, now empty save for a foul sludge that stained the rocks. "What has been unleashed upon our land, Thomas?"

The fisherman shook his head grimly. "I've no answers, lass, but we must sound the alarm. The village must be warned to take shelter inland."

Sarah nodded, finding her feet unsteadily. Together they hurried back up the beach. Just then, a cry split the sky—but not the haunting shriek they feared. An eagle soared overhead, wings outstretched as if guiding them home.

They gathered what villagers they found, relaying all they'd witnessed in urgent, fearful tones. The people murmured darkly, grasping children close. The parish priest, Father Michael, agreed to ring the warning bells.

That evening found them huddled inside the church, praying for deliverance as the bells' ominous clanging carried on the wind. Through stained glass windows, they watched night fall in an unnatural gloom. Strange lights flickered just beyond the dunes.

In the small hours, a crashing boom shook the chapel walls. Terror-stricken sobs arose from the crowd. But as suddenly as it came, the sound passed, leaving an thick, nauseating pall that stung their eyes and throats.

As dawn's pale light filtered in, it revealed gaunt, hollow faces. They had survived the night. But all knew the true test still lay ahead, when the morning tide rolled back in, and whatever curse had come upon the land was loosed once more upon the frightened shore.

When morning came, the villagers ventured from the church in silence. A thin mist rolled across the land under an overcast sky. As they picked their way down to the shore, foul smells assailed their noses.

The tideline was littered with tangled piles of seaweed and debris. Among the flotsam lay the battered corpses of fish and crabs. Others writhed feebly, covered in glistening boils.

Fionn, the boldest of the young men, waded out for a closer look. He suddenly gave a strangled yell and lurched back, nearly falling in his haste. Clutched in his hand was a nightmarish thing—a thick tentacle ending in barbed hooks that dripped some burning fluid.

The crowd shuddered as one. Thomas stepped forward, face grim. "We'll find no answers hiding ashore. I'm away to the boat and survey the depths." Despite protests, his mind was made up.

Sarah grabbed his arm. "Then I'm coming too. An extra pair of eyes may help." Thomas looked ready to refuse, but knew time was critical. They pushed off in wary silence.

Scanning the waters, at first they saw nothing untoward. Then Sarah cried out, pointing to an orange glint below. As they drew nearer, shapes twisted in the murk—gleaming carapaces, serrated fins, crawling legs of nightmare proportion.

Thomas reefed the sails as they drifted above the lurking forms. Sarah peered into the briny depths, straining to make out details through the turbid water.

The creatures milled about in no discernible pattern, congregating in patches then dispersing. Many bore ragged wounds that clouded the water with ink. As she watched, a hulking shape lashed out with limb-like appendages, seizing a smaller monster in a macabre waltz. Both disappeared into a roiling mass of slashing claws and snapping jaws.

A bubble of air escaped Sarah's lips in a soundless scream. Thomas placed a steadying hand on her shoulder, his weathered features grim. "This is no natural place, lass. Some evil has stirred these dark depths."

As if in reply, a thunderous boom shook the surf. A geyser erupted nearby, spewing a writhing tangle of limbs and teeth. In its midst glowed two bulbous eyes that fixed upon the small boat, burning with alien malice.

The abomination shrieked, the sound reverberating in their skulls. Its fellows answered with hisses and clicks that curdled the blood.

"We've seen enough!" cried Thomas, throwing his weight against the tiller. But as the boat lurched, a rippling shadow broke the surface directly beneath—something colossal, shifting in the gloom below their very keel.

Sarah stifled a scream as an immense, chitinous limb erupted from the depths, smashing down where the boat had been only moments before. Thomas swore and wrestled with the tiller, trying to put distance between them and the monstrosity below.

All around, the waters churned with movement as more twisted forms converged on their tiny craft. Sarah spotted glimmering eyes and snapping claws just beneath the roiling surf. "There's too many, we'll never outrun them!" she cried in panic.

Thomas' eyes darted frantically across the scene, then widened as if struck by inspiration. "To the cliffs, fast as you can go!"

He gunned the engine and cut a sharp turn towards shore. The things below gave chase with incredible speed, closing the distance with frightening ease. Sarah watched their pursuers crash and writhe in the boat's turbulent wake.

With a deafening roar, the cliffs loomed before them. Thomas aimed straight for the jagged rocks, unmindful of the certain destruction that awaited if he mistimed their approach. At the last moment, he wrenched the tiller and they scraped snarling along the shelf.

Monsters surged into the shallows after them, only to smash themselves upon the unyielding stone. For the moment, they were safe—but trapped with the tide rolling in and no escape by sea. As Sarah and Thomas sat gasping, far darker questions lingered...

Sarah and Thomas huddled on the narrow clifftop as the tide rushed in, cutting off their sole escape route. Below, the monsters milled in confusion, unable to pursue onto the rock shelf but unwilling to retreat. Their alien cries drifted eerily on the salt air.

"What devilry is this?" Thomas whispered in fear and dismay. Sarah could only shake her head mutely, eyes fixed on the surreal scene unfolding below.

As the tide peaked, the creatures' behaviorchanged. They began clustering together, merging into one giant pulsing mass. Sarah realized with horror what was transpiring - the monsters were breeding, coupling in a chaotic orgy of slapping flesh and flashing limbs.

A thunderous cracking split the air as a colossal form began tearing free of the merged conglomeration. Slime and gore flew as the abomination strained to liberate itself, like a bird breaking from an eggshell. With impossible speed, two more gargantuan beasts followed, already battling with inky tendrils that whipped and flailed.

Sarah glanced at Thomas, whose face had gone bone white. They both knew - these larger monsters could now easily scale the cliffs. As the trio of colossi turned glowing eyes upwards, hungry clicks emanating from unseen maws, Sarah steeled herself for the fight to come.

Whatever evils had been unleashed on this land, she and Thomas would stand against them with every ounce of strength and courage remaining.

The towering creatures reached cavernous limbs onto the cliff shelf, slathering the rocks with foul ichor. Sarah backed slowly across the narrow ledge, eyes darting for any means of escape or defense. Her hand closed around a jagged chunk of shale.

Beside her, Thomas brandished his hunting knife with a defiant yell. His courage heartened Sarah, and she faced the looming beasts with new resolve.

As grasping limbs crept closer, Thomas shouted "For home and hearth!" and charged with a wordless battle cry. He slipped past snapping claws and buried the knife hilt-deep in a rubbery eye. It shrieked in pain, thrashing wildly.

Sarah hurled her stone, cracking the other eye of a second monster just before it closed taloned fingers around Thomas. Now blind, it staggered—and tumbled screeching from the cliff.

The third abomination loomed over them, drooling corruption. With a crack of stone, its armored skull was split open from above. It crumpled, revealing Fionn and two other stalwart villagers atop the bluff.

Fionn tossed down a rope. "Hurry, the tide's rising fast!" As Sarah and Thomas clambered free of the surf's reach, behind them the cove erupted into a cacophony of war as man and monster met in savage battle upon the blood-slick rocks below.Hope had come, but the true war for their land had only just begun.

With Fionn's aid, Sarah and Thomas made it over the cliffs just as the next wave crashed through, washing some grotesque remnants of the battle out to sea. They collapsed, breathing hard, as their saviors hauled up the rope behind them.

Through the haze of exhaustion, Sarah heard Father Michael's voice. "The Lord be praised, you yet live. Now come - we must away from this accursed place."

She looked back one last time at the cove, now a charnel ground where unnatural tides ebbed and flowed. Though bloodied, the village men stood tall above their fallen foes, a hard-won victory. Still, she knew the real battle for their home had only begun.

That night as they took shelter inland, Sarah watched the glow of bonfires along the shore and heard the ragged cheers of men keeping watch. Despite losses and horrors, a new resolve had been forged among her people - they would stand united against the evil that had come, no matter the cost.

In quiet moments, Sarah took comfort knowing brave souls like Fionn, Thomas and the others stood between her village and the nameless terrors lurking in the depths. But she also knew that dark days were still ahead, and before long she too would have to take up the fight to reclaim their land. The war to come would try their souls to the very brink of endurance.

Something's Not Right

The next morning, Sarah awoke with the dawn. After surviving the terrors of the previous days, a restless tension gripped the village that no amount of prayer or whiskey seemed to ease.

She rose and began her chores, hoping the familiar routine might provide solace. But as the sun climbed, an unnatural malaise seemed to hang over the land. Birds sang half-heartedly among the pines, and not a breath of wind stirred the heather.

Looking out to sea did little to lift her mood. The waters lay as flat and still as a sheet of slate, revealing nothing of what might lie beneath. An eerie glow shimmered just at the edge of sight, like the flickering flame of a spent candle.

At mid-morning while feeding her goats, Sarah heard shouts from the village headman. Abandoning her pail, she raced down to find the people gathered in fearful clusters, pointing to the sky in the northeast.

Straining her eyes, Sarah gasped. On the bare hilltops along the coast a pallid mist had gathered, limned from within by an eldritch radiance. Pale tendrils reached down into the valleys like seeking fingers.

The priest stepped forward, face drawn. "Such unholy vapors portend only ill. We must away inland, away from these cursed shores, while strength yet remains to flee."

A gruff voice answered. "And leave our homes to the mercy of devils? Nay, Father, we'll stand our ground!" It was Thomas, face set in grim determination.

A nervous murmur arose as people looked to each for guidance in their desperation. Sarah knew no easy answers would be found, only a hard road ahead under darkened skies. Whatever evil had manifest, its shadow now loomed over their whole land.

As debate swirled, Sarah spied Fionn striding from his hut with sword in hand. She hurried to his side. "What is your counsel, friend?"

Fionn gazed at the ominous mists, lips pressed thin. "This evil aims to drive us from our homes like vermin. But we are not mice to flee at its coming! I say send scouts to learn our foe, while those able take up hammer and nail."

Sarah nodded firmly. "Well spoken. I'll gather all who can wield tool or blade to strengthen our defences, if Father Michael will bless the work."

The priest sighed wearily, but placed a hand on Fionn's shoulder. "Go with God's speed, my son. And may your sword arm be guided by mercy alone."

As scouts mustered their horses, Sarah organized villagers into work crews. Under Fionn's direction, defensive walls rose around the settlement. Others reinforced doors and windows, making even the smallest homes into potential bastions.

By sunset, when faint glows writhed in the mists like ghost lights, the village presented a united front against the shadows gathering beyond. But as Sarah banked the hearth fire for the night, an ominous silence reigned where once birds and insects sang. Whatever evil approached, she knew its coming would shake the land.

That night, an eerie mist rolled in from the sea, blanketing the valley in fetid fog. Strange shapes seemed to twist and turn within its pale shroud, glimpsed only for a moment before dissolving back into the murk.

The village stayed awake, huddled in their refuges. All eyes were drawn repeatedly to the windows, hoping each wisp outside was merely drifts of moisture—yet dreading confirmation that something darker prowled near.

In those long dark hours, Sarah found solace tending the wounded from recent battles. Among them lay Griogair, a wizened fisherman, nursing awful burns. As she cleaned and wrapped his weeping flesh, he tossed fitfully.

"Lass...something comes," he rasped through parched lips. "I saw...in the deeps. Worse than any beast...a thing of shadow and teeth. It hunts us...feels our fear on the wind."

Sarah soothed him gently, though his ravings chilled her blood. She prayed his wounds did not poison his mind. But when joyous birdsong failed to greet the dawn, an ominous stillness reigned in the veil of mist.

Just then, shouts arose from the watch. Sarah raced to the palisade with others, dread clenching her heart. Through the fog, undefined shapes swayed and shuffled—a nightmare horde emerging from the whiteness.

With a blast of horn, the guards leapt into action. But no steel could fell these foes. For as the mist parted, an army of corruption shambled into the light.

Horror gripped the village as the mist withdrew to revealhuman corpses shambling inexorably forward. Skin hung slack from gaping wounds, faces were frozen in rictus grins, yet their eyesburned with dark intelligence.

An armored skeletonlunged, sword wheeling, but Fionn's blade took its head with a single blow. It crumbled into ash. Yet behind marched an ever growing host, features lost to decay but purpose unstoppable.

Thomas barked orders to bar the gates. Sarah helped the injured inside while healers prepared defenses. Griogair appeared, bearing a long knife despite his burns."The mist...a summoning. Their master comes!"

As the dead pressed in, an unseen dirge keened upon the sea wind, stirring memories of joy now twisted into agonies. Sanity started slipping, butSarah rallied her people with stern cries.

The wall's base was breached when a skeletal colossus materialized, twice man-height. Its fleshless laugh split eardrums. Sarah braced for the end, then screamed in warning - behind the giant, deeper horrors took shape in the mists.

Fionn leapt upon the giant, cleaving through spine with a two handed blow. As it fell, he thrust a torch into grinning jaws, setting the dead ablaze. "To arms, for loved ones still living!"

Villagers rallied in renewed defiance as the mists parted, revealing a nightmare beyond all thought unfolding at the shore.

Through swirling mists, the villagers gazed in horror upon a spectacle of madness unfolding upon the beach. Towering monstrosities with flesh of roiling shadow dueled in an orgy of violence, smashing boulders to rubble with casual sweeps.

Crashing waves disgorged still more abominations - twisted amalgamations of spawn and carrion, bearing human remains as dread trophies. They swarmed the battling titans in a chittering, clawing horde.

But arising above the chaos loomed the source of this nightmare - a colossus that blotted out the sky, featureless save for a gaping maw set in a contorted visage. From within echoes a maddening song that clawed at the mind, urging the dead and defiled to ever greater savageries.

Seeing the true scope of the incursion, Father Michael crossed himself. "This is no natural evil. We face a force that walks the shores of Hell itself!"

Thomas nodded grimly. "Then to Hell it shall be sent. Ready pots of oil - we'll light the bastards up." Despite madness outside, iron will held fast within the palisade.

Fionn bellowed a challenge to the dead army battering the gates. With a grim nod to Sarah, he swung them wide to charge into butchery once more. Beyond hope, the village stood alone between sanity and the abyss.

Fionn led the charge, hacking a bloody swath through rotting corpses. Villagers flanked him, hurling burning pitch to engulf the dead in flame.

Sarah tended the wounded under Father Michael's guard. Through the gates, a grisly mosaic unfolded - Fionn cleaving titanic jaws from a crawler, Thomas impaling shriekers upon the palisade spikes.

Beyond, monsters smashed in primordial fury upon the shore. With each impact, waves tossed fluttering remains onto the rocks. Sarah gagged at the sights, but kept healing through sheer defiance of the madness.

A tremor shook the earth as two colossi fell locked in combat. A torrent of gore drowned the sands, sending a hellish tide surging towards the village.

"Brace the gates!" Sarah cried in warning. They barred the portcullis just as a black flood crested the wall in glurping surges. Rotting flotsam battered the palisade under a deluge of decay.

A piercing keening rent the air, twisting minds to breaking. Through the mire, Sarah spied beyond and froze in terror - the colossus conductor had spied their struggles, and now turned its fell attentions upon the village itself.

As the fog parted, the villagers beheld a nightmare given form - the towering conduit of the chaos towered above the cliffs, visage twisted in unholy rapture. From its maw poured the maddening dirge that swelled the tide of hellish spawns. It lurched towards the settlement, each footfall sundering boulders. Villagers braced for annihilation beneath its looming shadow.

Then, Fionn bellowed a wordless cry and charged alone towards certain doom. His challenge gave new heart to the defenders - together, they might yet wound this agent of the abyss.

Oil pots flew, engulfing claw and carapace alike. Thomas loosed flaming arrows to blacken eyes beneath its malevolent gaze. As it reeled, Fionn leapt, cleaving through a grotesque knob at its breast.

Blood poured like wine from the deep. With final shrieks, the horde dissolved into the surf, pulled back into the depths by some hellish will. The skies cleared as the dirge died upon windswept cliffs.

Though the dead army had been routed, its master had marked this place. In the aftermath, all knew darker days yet lie ahead. But for now, the villagers dared hope they had shown these accursed shores that humanity would not yield to the terrors from the deep without a fight.

Chapter 02

CHANGES UNDER THE WAVES
SEARCHING FOR ANSWERS

The days that followed were uneasily calm. Patrols along the shore found no sign of further monster incursions, though the waters roiled with an ominous glow each night.

The village took shelter further inland, amid hastily constructed defenses of sharpened stakes and watchfires.

Sarah stood vigil with the others, scanning the darkness for any threat. Her mind churned with worries for her people and questions about the evil that had driven them from their homes. Sleep offered no respite, only fitful dreams of twisting shapes in the depths.

One morning, Thomas found Sarah staring blankly at the surf and placed a hand on her shoulder. "Troubles weigh heavy, lass, but dwelling on them won't solve naught. I'm away to the ruins today - mayhap answers can be found there of what brought this curse upon us."

Sarah turned to him gratefully. "Let me come with you. An extra pair of eyes could aid the search, and I've no stomach left for idleness."

Thomas nodded, and soon they set off together down the coastline. Strange mounds had risen from the tideline - piles of flotsam deposited by retreating tides. Among the wrack lay familiar fixtures now turned grim - lobster pots tangled with seaweed, boats smashed against jagged rocks. The shore felt unrecognizable.

Rounding a bend, the ruins of an ancient stone circle emerged from the dunes. Thomas and Sarah picked their way across the weathered bluffs. Once a place of primal power, now only lichen-stained stones remained among encroaching sands. A sense of melancholy hung in the air.

"Here is where our people first settled, aeons past," Thomas explained somberly. "If darkness lies somewhere, perhaps answers can be found in the ruins of our forebears..."

Within the stone circle, Sarah began searching for any clues among the weathered markings. Thomas inspected the outer perimeter.

After some time, Sarah spotted drawings etched into a large central boulder. Wiping away grime revealed depictions of sea life both familiar and bizarre. One caught her eye - a fiery, shifting form with curled limbs like hooks.

"Thomas, come see!" she called out. When he leaned in, recognition dawned. "The likeness of those devilish creatures we saw. But what does this mean?"

Thomas ran a hand over the archaic carvings, transfixed. "Legends speak of entities from the deep said to prize the souls of men. Perhaps a curse of old has been visited upon us once more."

As they puzzled over the images, a shout came from the bluff. They turned to see Fionn waving urgently from above. "Hurry, something comes! An evil in the tide!"

Grabbing what clues they could, Thomas and Sarah raced up the scree. Emerging atop the bluff, they beheld a grim sight - far out, twinkling lights could be seen rising from the depths, flickering in unnatural patterns beneath the waves.

Fionn gestured farther downcoast. "There! In the cove...God preserve us, what fresh devilry is this?" Peering through spray-lashed glass, they saw writhing shapes massing upon the shore once more.

The monsters had returned to their cursed land. And this time, they did not come alone...

"We must sound the alarm," said Thomas grimly.

Fionn nodded. "I'll ride for the village on Swift, may she fly as fast as her namesake!"

The young man raced off, sure-footed down the treacherous cliffs. Thomas turned to Sarah. "The stones may hold more meaning now. Grab what writing you can - we'll lead these devils on a chase while Fionn raises the alarm."

They hurried back to the ruin, where Sarah scrabbled to make rubbings of the ancient carvings. Below, the monsters dragged themselves from the surf in greater numbers than before, joined now by lesser abominations the size of dogs.

Thomas hefted a stout branch. "Come, let's be gone from here!"

Staying low to avoid notice, they stealthily picked their way inland across treacherous dunes. Behind, an eerie skittering rose as the creatures gave chase, drawn by some primordial urge.

The dunes gave way to twisted scrubland. Thomas doubled back, waving his improvised weapon to distract their pursuers. "This way, foul beings! Follow if you dare!"

The ruse worked - the monsters crashed after them singlemindedly through the brush. Thomas and Sarah pelted away, adrenaline giving wings to their feet. In the distance, they heard the first blaring notes of the alarm horns - Fionn had done his job. All that remained was to lead the abominations into the territory of men once more...

Weaving through the scrub, Thomas and Sarah stretched their lead over the lumbering beasts. But with each bend the monsters gained ground steadily, driven by feral instinct.

Ahead, the treeline rose from sprawling heathland. Thomas veered towards a stand of ancient oaks encircling a long-dry well. "There, the village defenses!"

As they bolted into the clearing, a hail of stones and spears rained down from the treetops onto the pursuing horde. Villagers swarmed from hiding, shouting war cries. The monsters shrieked and stumbled under the barrage, turning on each other in confusion.

Fionn rode up as Thomas and Sarah bent double, gasping. "You led them true - now the hunting begins!"

With desperate strength, the wounded creatures fought back savagely. But the villagers' newfound courage held firm. Step by step they herded the beasts backwards towards the treeline, blades and staves whirling in a deadly dance.

A colossal monster loomed over the fray, swiping villagers aside like dolls. But Fionn put spurs to Swift and they charged, the horse's iron-shod hooves crunching flesh. The beast tottered and fell, crushing two companions underneath.

Slowly, the last monsters were cornered and torn down by the avenging villagers. When the carnage ended, the survivors stood silent amid mangled heaps of flesh, catching their breath in the grim aftermath of battle. A bittersweet victory, but one which lifted their hopes.

Father Michael stepped into the clearing, reciting a prayer for the fallen. Though grieved by losses, the villagers took solace in each other's survival.

Thomas went to Sarah, laying a hand on her shoulder. "Courage and guile saw us through once more. Come, let's return to the village - our people will want to hear of all you saw."

As they made their way back, Sarah shared all she had learned - the ancient carvings within the stone circle, hinting at dark powers stirring in the deep. The villagers listened grimly but with new resolve. Though questions remained unanswered, uniting against the threat had rekindled their spirit.

That night, as Sarah took her watch from the treetops, she gazed out across the darkened land. Fires twinkled in the distance where sentries stood vigil, keeping the terrors of the deep at bay.

Somewhere beyond the waves, beneath moon and stars, nameless evils still lurked with designs on this shore. But her people would not yield their home without a fight. As long as courage and community held strong, there was hope yet to be found even in darkness' deepest deeps.

With vigilance and fellowship, they would face whatever terrors arose from the waves. Together, they would survive.

An Octopus Ally

Days passed with an uneasy calm along the coast. Patrols found no further sign of monsters emerging from the sea, though unease lingered like sea mists over the village.

One morning, Sarah joined the shorebound sentries as dawn lightened the east. A offshore kelp forest drifted lazily in the surf, concealing what lay below the waves. Sarah scanned the susurrating fronds warily.

A flash of motion caught her eye - something large glided between the fronds, stirring the seaweed in swirling patterns. Sarah nocked an arrow to her string, straining for a clearer glimpse.

The thing resolved into an immense octopus, its tentacles twisting elegantly through the kelp. But unlike any octopus Sarah knew, this one bore strange bioluminescent markings that pulsed softly along its skin.

As she watched transfixed, the octopus seemed to sense her gaze. It turned bulbous eyes towards the shore, regarding Sarah with an uncanny intelligence. After a long moment, it slowly raised one tentacle in a gentle wave.

Sarah lowered her bow, stunned. Before she could react further, Thomas approached behind her. "What is it, lass? Have you..." He trailed off at the sight before them.

A breeze shifted the kelp, and through the wavering fronds Sarah thought she glimpsed movement deeper in the forest - shadowy forms observing from the gloom. She turned to Thomas with a feeling of portent. "I think...this octopus may mean us no harm. Let us go and see."

Against all instinct, Sarah and Thomas waded into the surf towards the waiting giant. Beyond lay answers to what changes had come, for good or ill, beneath the watching waves...

As Sarah and Thomas waded out, the giant octopus remained motionless, regarding them calmly. Up close, its pale flesh was flecked with shimmering patterns in hues of blue and gold.

When the villagers were a pace away, it slowly extended a tentacle towards them. Thomas laid a cautious hand upon the slick appendage, marveling at its muscular contractions.

"Steady friend, your touch speaks of trust," said Sarah quietly. At her words, a flush of bioluminescence pulsed briefly across the octopus's skin in reply.

Thomas turned to her in awe. "It seems you've a gift, lass, to earn the trust of such a rare beast. Perhaps it can offer insights we sorely need."

Just then, gasps arose from the shore. Sarah glanced back to see the village elders approaching in a rowboat, led by Father Michael. When they beheld the octopus, expressions rippled from fear to wonder.

"Dark days are upon us, so ones said, when strange portents walk the land," intoned the priest. "This creature appears a sign we must heed. Let us bring it back and learn what knowledge dwells in ocean deeps."With care, Sarah and Thomas helped guide the giant cephalopod into the boat. It curled comfortably amidships, resting protective tentacles around the villagers as they rowed back to shore together.

A crowd had gathered, eyes widening at the sight of the immense octopus wending inland with the returning party. Sarah went among them, recounting all she had witnessed with a growing sense of revelation. Change was coming, borne on shifting tides...

That evening, the villagers gathered around the octopus, regarding it with curiosity and wonder. Father Michael offered a prayer of thanks for this gift from the sea.

Through gestures and bioluminescent flashes, the octopus seemed eager to communicate. Sarah found she could interpret its meanings intuitively. "It wishes to help us. There are powers stirring in the deep that threaten all who dwell here, human and creature alike."

Murmurs rose among the villagers. Fionn spoke up. "These shores have been home to octopi since time out of mind. What meaning do the markings on its skin hold?"

At the question, the octopus shifted its coloration, displaying intricate spirals and flowing lines across its body. Sarah gasped. "The patterns match the carvings in the ancient stones! It knows of the old powers that once dwell here."

Hope kindled in the crowd's eyes. If this creature understood the past, perhaps it could help divine their portentous future.

Night deepened around their commune. As villagers brought gifts of fish to their guest, Sarah felt a calling to learn all she could from the wellspring of wisdom before them. With the octopus's aid, mysteries of the deep might at last come to light.

But darker truths also lurked below the waves, and in time they would rise again to test this fragile bond between land and sea.

In the days that followed, Sarah spent long hours conversing with the giant octopus, gaining insight into the nature of its strange intelligence. Through gestures and flashes of colors, it told tales of elder gods dwelling in fathomless crevasses, and of corruption spreading through the currents from blasphemous depths.

Its wisdom shed new light on the carvings in stone, hinting at primal forces now awakening once more. The villagers listened intently as Sarah shared these revelations, drawing strength from newfound purpose - to stand against the invading darkness and protect their land.

Yet change was coming, as evidenced by the unthinkable cooperation of man and cephalopod. Sarah felt the ties between sea and shore realigning in ways not seen since time's dawn.

After many talks, the octopus informed Sarah through mournful pulses that it must soon return to the deep, though it promised to aid the villagers from the waters should threat arise again. On the morning of its departure, the entire village gathered to bid their strange ally farewell.

As its gleaming bulk slipped back into foaming waves, Sarah felt both loss and hope. With the octopus watching unseen from below, and the villagers standing vigil above, perhaps this land could endure the trials to come through courage, community - and unexpected friendships forged between depths and domes of sea and sky.

A Helping Hand

Weeks passed peacefully along the coast. While the villagers remained vigilant, no further sightings of monsters occurred. Still, an undercurrent of unease lingered like the fading echoes of old nightmares.

One morning, fisherman Thomas rowed his boat out at dawn's first light. He cast his nets, mending torn lines and thinking on the strangeness of recent days. A splash drew his gaze outward - through the mist, something moving.

As the fog parted, Thomas saw a small rowboat adrift, bearing a lone figure slumped at the stern. He rowed over in haste. "Hoy there! Are you injured?"

The person raised their head weakly - a young woman, pale and shaking. "Please...help...my village..." She collapsed once more.

Thomas hauled her into his boat. Her clothing was torn and she bore deep cuts, but still drew faint breath. He rowed hard for the shore, praying she could yet be saved. Breaking from the mist, his shouts rang across the beach.

Villagers raced to assist, laying the woman tenderly on furs. Father Michael knelt, checking for life signs. "She yet clings to this world, by God's grace. Quick now, to the healer's hut!"

As dawnlight strengthened, the villagers worked tirelessly to save the mysterious castaway. Would their efforts prove enough to earn some explanation for the dark events stirring once more beneath the waves?

Within the healer's hut, village wives worked to stabilize the wounded stranger. Father Michael called upon all his skills to tend her injuries.

After an anxious wait, the priest emerged wearily. "The danger has passed - she will live, though in a fragile state. Now we can but tend her rest and pray she finds strength to share her story in time."

Word spread quickly of the mysterious survivor. That evening, villagers gathered at the hut to offer supplies and well-wishes. Through the threshold, Sarah glimpsed the young woman lying pale as snow upon woven rolls.

In the nights that followed, fever ravaged the castaway as injuries fought to heal. Sarah took watch by firelight, gently wiping her brow. Finally, on the fourth night, the woman stirred from haunted dreams.

"Water..." she rasped weakly. Sarah held a skin to parched lips, then smiled down with quiet reassurance.

Slowly, awareness returned to haunted eyes. "You...saved me. My village..." Tears welled, spilling down ashen cheeks.

Sarah took the stranger's hand softly. "Be at peace - you are safe now. When strength returns, share your tale if you're able. For now, only rest."

The woman nodded gratefully, soon slipping back into a calm slumber under watchful eyes. Changes were unfolding once more in lands both below and above the waves, and with hope, this castaway's story would lend more pieces to the deepening mystery.

Over ensuing days, the castaway regained her strength bit by bit. Villagers lent encouragement, hoping in turn to learn the truth of what horrors had befallen her home.

At last, one afternoon, Sarah found her sitting upright beneath woven hides, pale face set in resignation. "I am ready now. My name is Aoife, daughter of the Sea Grove village headman. Please, gather your people - I would share my warning."

Word swiftly spread. As evening fell, villagers crowded anxiously within the longhouse, seating Aoife before the warmth of the central hearth. She began her tale in steady, haunted tones:

"All was well in Sea Grove until dark shapes began rising from the deep. Monstrous beings like none we'd seen, crawling ashore with murderous intent. They fell upon us without mercy..."

She told of horrors - homes torched, families torn asunder while the monsters fell upon her people like scavengers. Barely escaping with her life by taking to the tide-tossed boats.

"Days I drifted before washing ashore here. But what of the others - did any also survive? I pray the souls of Sea Grove have found peace, if the village itself now lies in ruins..."

She fell silent, eyes damp once more. Villagers shared haunted looks, dread mingling with quiet outrage at the fate of their neighbors. New resolve kindled in place of fear - they would stand united against the blight that had fallen from the sea.

A heavy silence fell as Aoife finished her grim tale. Then Father Michael rose, saying a solemn prayer for the souls of Sea Grove.

Villagers brought Aoife food and furs, tending her with care. Though grieving, she took comfort in their kindness to a stranger.

That night as Aoife slept, Sarah went to the healer. "Her warning echoes the octopus's portents. These horrors come not by chance, but by some darker power's design."

The healer nodded grave agreement. "We face a threat beyond experience. Your gift for ocean tongues may prove a light, as may this maiden's firsthand knowledge of assault from sea."

On the morrow, Aoife emerged stronger, ready to counsel the villagers on battling the monstrous foe. Though an outsider, she was welcomed as one of their own - for in standing together against the invading dark, lay their sole means of survival.

And so with Aoife's aid and the guidance of octopus allies below, the villagers began readying defenses against whatever terrors yet lurked in the deep, waiting to spread their blight upon the shore.

Glowing Wonders

As summer waned towards harvest, an uneasy peace held along the coast. Yet all knew darker seasons lay ahead, and with them threats unnamed.

One dawn, fisherman Thomas rowed out before the breakers, casting his nets where kelp forests drifted. A strange blue radiance caught his eye down floating strands - ghostly pinpricks bobbing in the surf.

Curious, he hooked a frond to haul closer. Floating amid fronds were tiny jellyfish, pulsing with inner glow like ephemeral lanterns. But their bell-shapes were intricate as snowflakes, delicate tendrils flowing elegantly within clear domes.

Thomas had never seen their like before. As he marvelled, more strange forms appeared below - translucent shells tinged aquamarine, flashing spines that mirrored sunlight in crystalline dazzle. Wondrous unknown life teeming in protected coves amid sun-dappled kelp.

Filled with wonder, Thomas hastily rowed to share his discovery. Word spread quickly bringing elders to the shore by dawn, eager to behold the gleaming bounties of deep revealed. They hoped glimpsing nature's mysteries might lend insights into greater riddles facing their kinfolk.

Sure enough, crested heads soon emerged from tents and longhouses to gather expectantly upon the surf-scoured sands. What uncanny marvels had the tides delivered this morn, and what forestallings of future fortunes might they contain?

As the elders arrived, Thomas waded out to the kelp line, carefully hauling ghostly specimens ashore in woven nets. Gasps arose at the bounty revealed - creatures like none seen before, bioluminescent forms casting soft azure radiance even in day's warm light.

Father Michael breathed a prayer of wonder. "Who can fathom the hidden glories of the Lord's creation? Some work here may shed light on greater riddles facing us."

The healer Sarah gently cradled a gem-like shell, tracing spiraling ridges. "Exquisite adaptations - these thrive unseen amid protection. As do we by standing together against darkness."

Their visitor Aoife leaned close, eye alight. "In Sea Grove's trading, we exchanged crafts for curios from the deep. Such rarities fetch high prices from big city alchemists."

This gave elders pause. The village economy relied on seasonal trade, but losing their protectors to risky travels seemed ill-advised now. Risking the welfare of villagers for coin felt a poor exchange.

As discussion continued, Sarah approached bearing a cradle of jellyfish, glowing softly within. "These pulse in harmony with the tides' ebb and flow. Perhaps they may aid my studies of the sea..."

An idea was taking shape - to glean what wisdom nature offered, yet safeguard people above all else in these uncertain times.

That evening, elders gathered in council longhouse to discuss using their finds wisely.

Father Michael began. "These gifts could lift people's spirits, yet selling abroad risks losing protectors. Another path lies open - teach craft to honour gifts from sea, as seafolk honour gifts from land."

Sarah agreed. "My studies show alchemical uses - dyes, illuminants, even medicines perhaps. But skills must grow with care, not haste."

Thomas spoke next. "Seeing wonders of shore inspired folk. Keeping finds safe here, sharing crafts' joy, may light hope's flame when darkness looms."

Sarah smiled. "My talks with octopus friend hinted at deeper harmonies 'tween all beings, seen and unseen. Honouring these with reverence and respect could strengthen fragile bonds we'll need."

Aoife affirmed. "Sea Grove folk bartered wide, yet valued community above all. Your way honours both gifts and givers, as people and spirits of land and sea."

A consensus formed - to foster crafts celebrating gifts from tide and keep all finds within protectors' watch, sharing joys of discovery as darkness ebbed in seasons to come. New purpose blossomed to face trials ahead through reverence, resilience and community's strength.

With the plan set, work began in earnest. Sarah's apprentices gathered samples, studying glows and properties under wise guidance.

Sarah met often with the village children, introducing wondrous finds and their unseen neighbors below the waves. Eyes widened at sparkling shells cradling bioluminescent forms, kindling curiosity about intricate balances of shore and sea.

Weavers and artisans experimented with dyes, capturing flashes of color seen only in secret niches. Thomas and the fisherfolk worked together to record rhythms observed, using songs and stories to share unfolding understanding.

Through these studies, legends emerged - of ancestral pacts with ocean spirits, primal bonds between all beings great and small. Villagers drew strength renewing ties to the land and its guardians, seen and unseen.

As harvest season ended and nights drew in, completed works were unveiled. Wool, linen and leather were dyed indigo and azure, glimmering softly like waves at dusk. And shining in Sarah's hut, stored samples offered steady illumination through long nights.

Laughter and music echoed in the feasting hall that eve, hearts lighter facing season's deepening mysteries together, gifts from sea and shore embraced. Through creativity and discovery, darkness held less power over souls of coast and village folk.

Under cover of gathering moonlight, the villagers' works were shared - shawls and tunics dyed with subtle radiance, vials of glowing solutions crafted through care and study. Gasps of wonder filled the hall at such transformations.

As celebrations wound down, Sarah took Aoife aside. "Your aid has been invaluable to us. But what now of your own path, once healed?"

Aoife smiled sadly. "Sea Grove can never be reclaimed. But another village yet clings to coast farther north - folk who traded with mine own. I would find if any also survived..."

She trailed off uncertain. Sarah grasped her hands warmly. "Then you need travel no farther alone. When spring thaws the passes, my people will stand with you."

Heart swelling, Aoife embraced her new friend. Through shared trials, fragile bonds of community had strengthened where once was only fearsome solitude.

And so as night fell and villagers retired to rest, a glimmer of hope remained. Though darker seasons surely lay ahead, with care and reverence for gifts of land and sea, this village's spirit yet endured - standing as testament to the power of sheltering one another through unity against whatever storms approached from the deep.

***

Chapter 03

SPREAD OF STRANGE POWERS

SAMPLES AND SECRETS

Winter fell heavily upon the village as the year drew to a close. Skies wept endless tears of ice and through piercing winds, the sea's roar seemed a distant memory.

Within the safe haven of Sarah's hut, studies of shore's gifts continued through the harshest moons. Under the healer's guidance, samples gathered that fateful morn were carefully cataloged and their myriad mysteries probed.

Through patient observation, curious properties were revealed. Some organisms pulsed in lovely harmony with lunar phases, shedding subtle radiances each night. Others responded to temperatures, glowing brightly when warmed gently between fingertips.

Most intriguing of all were filaments found deep in kelp fronds, encased in translucent pods pulsing with an inner blue radiance that seemed sustained without need for sun or sea. What strange font of power lay within, fueling their perpetual glow?

As clouds gathered for another winter gale, Sarah called her apprentices close. "While secrets of moon and tide are known, this last mystery begs further study. With care and wisdom, we may glean gifts to help folk when storms hold sway."

Under the healer's guidance, the apprentices began devising experiments to test their hypotheses regarding the luminous pods' source. Some tested effects of temperature and light, while others studied responses to stimuli like touch or disturbance in fluids. Through diligent yet respectful observation, their understanding slowly deepened...

Weeks passed as the apprentices worked, careful not to damage the delicate pods. Then one evening, the youngest noticed something strange.

"Sarah, come see! When I placed two pods together in water, their glow grew stronger."

The healer peered closely. Sure enough, a pulsating light emanated from where the pods touched. "Fascinating. Fetch the catalog - let us test this with others."

One by one, different pods were paired as the others watched with bated breath. Time and again, contact sparked a brighter radiance that built upon each pairing. A theory took shape - some synergistic process amplified the glow.

But when pods touched skin, no reaction occurred. Sarah pondered this late into the night, until a startling realization struck - could their very life energies fuel this photic alchemy?

The next attempt was dared only with greatest care. As two pods were brought together below the water's surface, a gasp rose - pure aquamarine light flared where they met, strong as daylight beneath clear waves.

Something profound had been discovered. But what implications did this hold, if simple contact between living things could spark such shows of luminance and power?

Word of the discovery spread quickly through the village. The elders gathered at Sarah's hut, eyes alight with wonder and concern.

"What mystical force resides in these pods, that contact alone amplifies their inner glow?" mused Father Michael.

Sarah responded carefully. "Some deep synergy exists between their life essence and ours. But we must take care - powers we don't understand could have unforeseen consequences if misused."

Thomas nodded slowly. "Like flame, this gift could light our way or burn if left to spread unchecked. Wisdom is finding balance."

Aoife spoke up. "In my village's past, we were warned of such curiosities washing ashore. Contact was said to 'wake what sleeps,' drawing attention from the deep..."

A chill fell over the group at her ominous words. Sarah broke the silence. "My octopus friend senses changes far below, but nothing yet comes into focus. For now, all we can do is observe and protect these mysteries as best we may."

A somber consensus formed - more study was needed, with utmost care and vigilance. For who knew what strange new forces were unfolding across the land and seas, and how their village might be impacted?

Winter deepened as the villagers kept close watch, hoping no further changes arose under waves or within woodland groves.

In Sarah's hut, the apprentices' diligent yet cautious work continued. Through experiments pairing different samples, properties were mapped and wonders catalogued for future safekeeping of knowledge.

All found took care handling the mystifying pods, harnessing their luminal synergy only to shed subtle light through the harshest snows. Touch alone could spark unforeseen repercussions, so contact was avoided save under guidance of weathered elders.

And so in vigilance and reverence, the village weathered that long winter bearing down. Through sharing finds yet protecting fragile balances, community bonds were strengthened enough to shelter all from whatever stranger tides might flow when spring's thaw set in.

None could say what changes further lay in store, across the lands and seas their fates were tied to. All that could be done was brace together, study nature's gifts, and pray dawn of a new season brought hope not further ill portent from the deep green waters of the unknown.

A Bountiful Catch

Spring's return swept away winter's chill but left unrest in its wake. Strange happenings were noted as thaw set in - plants budding weeks early, flocks migrating without pattern through skies.

In the woodlands strange tracks appeared, tracing circles around ancient trees glowing softly at dusk. None could name the creatures that left such marks, if creatures at all they were

Unease grew in the village as natural cycles seemed disrupted. But with warming seas came the promise of abundant harvest, and so fishing boats prepared to ply waves once more.

One morn Thomas and three others set out as mists still hung low. Further than usual they rowed, hoping richer cod banks might lift village spirits.

Breaking fog, a gasp rose - schools stretched as far as eye could see, silver glint flooding the sea. Nets sank, bursting with writhing bounty. Baffled but grateful, men hauled over burdens three times typical yield.

What force had congregated such astonishing plenty? Returning ashore, crowds gathered clutching offerings to the sky, grateful yet fearful of mysteries in the deep...

Upon pulling their boats ashore, Thomas and the others were met with exclamations of awe and worry from the gathered villagers.

"Never have the waters borne such riches!" called one man.

"But is this nature's gift, or some omen?" fretted an elderly woman.

News of the massive catch soon reached Sarah, who went down to the beach to examine the findings for herself. She saw how the cod were packed impossibly tight in the nets, as if forcefully driven together.

Turning to Thomas, she asked "Did you notice anything strange upon the waters?"

Thomas shook his head. "Only a queer glow beneath the waves at the schools' edges. As if circling an invisible flame."

Overhearing, Aoife spoke up nervously. "In my village's past, unnatural bounties preceded times of upheaval. We must discern if this bodes well or ill..."

At this, murmurs of worry spread through the crowd. Father Michael called for calm. "Speculation breeds only fear. Let us seek wisdom through observerance and prayer."

Sarah nodded. "This gift feeds our people, but its cause raises questions. I'll study samples for signs, while you prepare the catch. We'll convene at dusk to share findings."

And so work began to portion the miraculous haul, though an air of unease lingered as mysteries deepened beneath the waves.

That evening, villagers gathered in the longhouse to share what had been learned. Sarah began by displaying shells and flesh she had examined under her microscope.

"The cod seem otherwise healthy, but traces were found on their skins - as if tiny fragments clung that pulsed with an internal luminance. I've never seen aught like it in all my years."

Thomas spoke next. "While readying the catch, I noticed the same fragments drifting in buckets of water. When two touches, their glow strengthened like the pods from winter studies."

Sarah grew pensive. "Could these fragments hail from those strange organisms? And do they somehow lure or drive the fish in vast numbers?"

Aoife nodded slowly. "Dark whispers from my past speak of 'lights in the deep' herding prey toward unseen predators. But what force draws these fragments to the surface?"

Silence fell as all pondered this unnerving possibility. Then a soft voice spoke - one of the children who had been listening intently.

"If the fragments glow where they meet, maybe they call to each other across the sea. Like a signal drawing all together toward the shore..."

The elders exchanged wary looks at this innocent yet chilling hypothesis. Further mysteries were unfolding in thedeep, and their implications remained perilously unclear.

That night, an uncanny luminosity was seen pulsing just beyond the surf - as if myriad tiny lights were communicating offshore in wordless chorus.

Though the catch had fed their people, an air of disquiet hung over the village. Forces beyond understanding seemed to be stirring, heralded by unnatural tides that could either bless or curse depending on currents not their own.

In coming days, patrols would walk the strand after dusk, watching for any signs or portents in the gloaming phosphoresence. Messages might yet be gleaned, if sensed with wisdom, empathy and care.

Sarah too observed longer than most, hoping science and spirit working in tandem could fathom what awoke beneath the waves. For now, all that could be known was that mysteries were deepening, strings tying their fates to powers unseen were tightening, and calmer waters may not flow again soon.

All folk could do was hold fast to community, guard kindred gentleness of spirit, and pray understanding of nature's way would guide them safe to springtimes yet to come.

A Smarter Sea

As days grew longer, disquiet spread through the village. Strange happenings now occurred daily - fish leaping from waters to avoid some unseen pursuer, flocks scattering at random across the sky.

Most unsettling were reports from offshore - lobster pots left untended emerged from the sea completely empty, as if every crustacean had vanished at once. Were the creatures of shore and sea becoming wiser to man's devices?

One morning, Thomas prepared to venture out once more, this time alone to check crab traps set the evening prior. He prayed for at least a modest catch to provision the village even a little.

Breaking surf, a startled shout - every single trap floated open and empty on the waves. Frantically peering below revealed none of the usual scuttling forms tangled within. Only drifting glimmers hinted at some lingering presence...

Thoroughly unnerved, Thomas pulled for shore with all haste, shouting a warning as wreckage of sea-life and normalcy continued washing between the worlds of air and deep. What change was rippling through the blue wilderness beyond sight that now even simplest harvests were denied?

Upon reaching the shore, Thomas gathered the villagers in a panic. "The traps were all emptied as if by invisible hands! Not a crab could be found though they were full at dusk. Some magic is at work out there!"

Unease turned to fear among the crowd. Aoife spoke grimly, "When the sea grows this clever, it often means larger hunters prowl just below the waves."

Before panic could set in, Sarah called for calm. "Speculation will not answer our needs. We must understand this new intelligence at play." She turned to Thomas. "Take me to where you set the traps. Perhaps there I can find clues."

They rowed to the spot and searched the waters. At first nothing seemed amiss, but then Sarah spotted dots of light swirling in the depths. She delved beneath and emerged with a glowing fragment.

"This residue was left behind, similar to what we saw on the cod. Could these fragments somehow enhance awareness of all sea life, enabling it to outwit our traps?"

Her question hung heavy with implications. If the sea grew too clever, how would the village survive? They needed answers, and quickly, before this strange power changed the balance entirely.

That evening, the elders gathered once more in urgent discussion. Sarah had been studying the fragment she retrieved, and her findings only deepened the troubling mysteries.

"Through my microscope, I've observed these residues seem to pulse with an intelligence of their own," she began. "When isolated, their glow is muted - but place two together, and they communicate swiftly inatterns beyond our understanding."

Thomas ran a hand through his hair anxiously. "Could it be...these fragments have spread throughout the sea, allowing all within to converse as one mind? Explaining why traps go untouched and fish now sense us coming?"

Murmurs of fear ran through the group at such a prospect. Aoife interjected grimly, "In the old stories, whenever the deep grows cunning, a new hunter has claimed dominion beneath the waves. But what manner of beast releases such witchery?"

Before panic could take hold, Father Michael spoke. "Despair and fear solve nothing. We must counter this change with calm action. I suggest tomorrow we try luring fragments aboard, to study their nature and passage more."

A tentative plan was forged as uncertainty loomed vast as the ocean itself. By what means could they solve this riddle, before the mystery remaining offshore swallowed their lives entirely?

At dawn, a small group set out in a boat carrying buckets of water from the sea. Hoping to attract any luminous fragments drifting near, they slowly rowed from the village outskirts, scanning the waters.

For hours nothing was seen. But as the sun reached its zenith, Thomas cried out - just below, pinpricks of light swirled as if communicating. Sarah carefully submerged a bucket.

To their amazement, the fragments began streaming toward the vessel, dancing upon the surface in their dozens. Quickly pulling the bucket up, they beheld the waters within aglow with a shifting, pulsating presence.

Sarah examined the spectacle closely. "See how they call to each other - every new addition strengthens the whole. As if sharing some collective intelligence across the sea."

Her words unsettled the others. What manner of entity used such sorcery to enhance all marine life? Was it protecting its domain, or pursuing darker ends?

Before anxiety overwhelmed them, Father Michael suggested returning to shore. But as they turned the boat, a massive shadow passed deep below. An awed silence fell - had they disturbed some colossal presence, or guardian of the deep?

Casting wary eyes across the waves, all hurried home, questions mounting heavier than any catch. What manner of change was rippling through kingdom blue?

That evening, as sunset painted sea and sky crimson, the village elders met once more by Sarah's hut.

She recounted all that was witnessed upon the waters that day. The fragments' communal glow, the vast shape sensed below, hinted at changes of unprecedented scale unfolding in the depths.

Aoife said grimly, "Old stories speak of a time when a new leviathan rose, warping tides and driving lesser beasts before it. Could something similar now emerge, using alien magic to remake the blue wilderness in its image?"

Fear gripped the group at such a prospect. But Father Michael counselled hope. "While mysteries deepen, doom is not assured. Through vigilance and care for nature's balance, as in past upheavals, perhaps a new understanding can still be reached."

In the days ahead, patrols would walk the glimmering strands ever watchful for signs. And Sarah vowed to study fragments, tracking their spread and influence, searching for insight that might safeguard peoples yet drawn too near some vast transition unfolding in kingdom blue.

For now, all that could be done was wait, observe, and pray new awareness would dawn before changes wrought by the awakening deep proved too immense to weather safely through storms lapping ever nearer the shores.

Watching From Within

That night, the fragments' ethereal glow pulsed more vibrant along the shore than ever witnessed before. Anxieties grew in the village as citizens kept vigil, hoping their presence would not draw some monstrous attention from below.

In her hut, Sarah studied fragments she had carefully stored in glass vials. Seeking to pierce their mysteries, she administered fluids extracted from local plant and animal life, observing responses through her microscope.

To her fascination, the fragments reacted strongly - pulses grew faster, patterns more complex, as if "conversing" with introduced samples on a molecular level. Had she found a means to commune, and possibly reason with, the strange Presence awakened in the deep?Eager to share her findings, yet wary of raising hopes too high, Sarah convened the elders at dawn. As they gathered, an urgent cry arose - a light had been seen ashore, creeping towards the woods under cover of mists.

Steadying nerves, the group readied to give chase, and hopefully gain more insight into the changes unfolding around them.

Sarah gathered several vials of fragments and reagents while the others readied boats and provisions. After briefing the village healer to care for any wounded, the group set off along the shoreline.

Climbing from their boats, all strained eyes and ears for any sign of the mysterious glow. For hours nothing was found amidst the fog-shrouded woods. Just as hope was fading, Aoife's keen sight spotted a glimmer deep within the trees.

Cautiously advancing, a hushed gasp arose - a fragment, larger than any seen, pulsed upon the moist earth, sending tendrils of light winding amongst the roots of an ancient yew. Sarah carefully administered a reagent vial.

To their amazement, the fragment's response was euphoric - lights intensified and spun in a dizzying dance. Had contact been made with the vast collective consciousness dwelling offshore? If so, what revelations might be gained by continuing communication?

Heartbeats quickened as possibilities, and perils, of interacting with the awakened Presence grew vast beyond imagining. Cautiously, Sarah prepared to inquire what changes stormed the shores, and what bridges could be built between two worlds drawn suddenly, and uncertainly, together.

With hands trembling in wonder and worry, Sarah administered another reagent and addressed the shimmering fragment:

"We mean no harm, only to understand. What great Presence calls the tides, and why come your lights ashore?"

The fragment's flashing seemed to quicken in thought. Then pulses formed distinct, repeating patterns that brought gasps."It understands! And responds!" cried Thomas.

Sarah watched keenly. "The pulses...they resemble cod markings we've seen. As if recalling when first the fragments came."

Hope and fear filled all present. Had contact been made with the mysterious intelligence awakening the seas? What desires and designs lay behind the changes shaking shores and deeps?

Sarah tried again. "We wish only to live in balance. How may peoples of land and sea do so, as storms gather fast beyond our sight?"

Flashing paused, as if considering. Then a message came, chilling all present with its clarity:

"All must change or perish, as One awakens to claim reign once more..."

What fate did this portend for those of shore and blue wilderness beyond? The scholars knew not, but sensed vaster dramas unfolding than any could have imagined.

A heavy silence fell over the group as the implications of the message sank in. Whatever primordial entity was stirring in the deep, its rise heralded changes that could reshape the very face of the world they knew.

Sarah addressed the fragment again, hoping to convey their goodwill. "We mean no challenge to dominion of the seas. Only to safeguard peoples if this 'One' awakens fully. Is there no cooperation between our kinds?"

The fragment pulsed for a long moment. Finally, a reply came. "Change is the way of the wild deep. Adapt or be left behind as tides shift. But know that all life is connected - harm one, harm all. Preserve balance if you would weather rising storm."

With that cryptic warning, the fragment's lights began to fade. Swiftly Sarah administered a final reagent, preserving its essence for further study.

As mists rolled in, the group retreated silently to shore, minds whirling with all they had witnessed and learned. While hope remained that understanding with the mysterious entity could be found, clearer now was the scale of transition reshaping the blue dominion, and all who dwell within its surrounds. Only vigilance and care for balance in trying times would see them through challenges lapping ever closer to the sands they called home.

***

Chapter 04

ESCALATING EVOLUTION

Hunters on the Hunt

News of the fragment encounter spread fast through the village, renewing unease. It seemed forces far greater than themselves were stirring in waters once familiar, and change would come to shore whether folk were prepared or not.

Uncertainty reigned for days as waves continued glittering with mystery each night. Then one morn, shouts rang out - a great tail fin had been spotted breaking swells far offshore, bigger than any whale. Was something colossal awakening in the deep?

Before speculation could grow wild, a hunting party from the neighboring village of Inver rushed in, out of breath.

"Our boats were attacked at dawn!" cried their leader Brennan. "Sea life like none seen - huge barbed forms breaking surface. We only barely made escape!"

Gasps arose at such a tale. Aoife asked grimly, "Attacks by strange beasts so close to shore - is evolution running rampant under waves, unrestrained by any known law of nature?"

Dark thoughts filled all, until Sarah called for reason. She turned to the hunters. "Take me to where you were set upon. Perhaps clues there can shed light on what transformation is unfolding in the deep..."

Brennan and his party rowed Sarah swiftly to site of the attack. As they neared, trails of disintegrating skin and innards stained swells – remnants of prey overwhelmed by savage force.

Examining remains, Sarah exclaimed, "Gills not seen on any creature before! As if evolved for transition between water and air!"

Thomas blanched. "Over generations, fragments' power seeps into sea life's very code. Driving change far beyond normal bounds..."

Upon speaking, a massive shadow passed deep below, dwarfing all present. Huntsman O'Conner cried, "Look! Like a mountain it moves!"

All froze as a colossal, saw-toothed maw breached the surface, snapping closed where remaining gore drifted. Its armored hide glinted with an unnatural sheen under the sun.

Before anyone could react, the leviathan sounded, disappearing into the murky depths. An awestruck hush fell over group as magnitude of transformation unfolding in the deep truly sank in.

With pounding hearts, the group slowly made way back to shore. All remained silent, minds reeling from the titanic scale of the beast glimpsed below.

Upon landing, Sarah immediately gathered the village elders. "What I have witnessed exceeds any natural development," she began solemnly. "Through fragments' enhancement, evolution within the seas is accelerating unchecked into frightening new terrain."

Murmurs of fear arose at such grim portents. Aoife added darkly, "And if lands above also bear fragments' taint upon the wind, who knows what twisted forms may arise to challenge dominion of sky and field?"

Panic threatened to take hold, until Thomas spoke. "Despair helps none. We must understand how fragments' power has permeated all domains. Only then can proper steps be taken to safeguard change shaping both our worlds."

All saw wisdom in his words. Resolve grew to deepen surveillance of forest, field and shore, tracking fragments' infiltration and life's responses. Yet as patrols gathered their gear and provisions, would they find changes already too extensive to counter without drastic action?

And how long until transformations spilled from sea to disrupt all in their wake? Grave hours were falling.

That evening, Sarah concluded further study of the slain beasts' remains. Her findings only deepened fears - fibrous tissue and sensory clusters unlike any species, almost machinelike in complexity.

She addressed the somber village. "Through fragments' enhancement, evolution ventures where no life has gone before. These creatures show early signs of adapting to walk on land."

Gasps arose at such a dire portent. Thomas spoke grimly, "If sea life gains footing on our shores, what defense have we? Especially if land animals also mutate into terrifying new forms?"

Before terror took hold, Father Michael urged hope. "While dangers mount, all is not lost. So long as fragments' spread is contained and balance preserved, perhaps worse changes can be stayed."

Seeking solutions, the elders proposed round-the-clock patrols of coast and forest. Any anomalous wildlife would be carefully tracked and, if needed, destroyed beforemutations could spread further.

Yet as dawn broke on the first surveillance missions, would watchers find changes already too vast to curtail without unleashing fiercer forces none had foreseen? For fragments' influence was permeating all domains in alien ways, and evolution's alteration accelerated towards unknown shores.

And so the watch began in earnest. Small patrol groups fanned out across shorelines, cliffs and forest trails at all hours, scanning for any signs of abnormality.

For weeks nothing out of the ordinary was seen. But as skies darkened on the 30th night, shouts rang out from western sentries - along the tideline lay strange footprints, far too large to be any known creature's.

Dawn's light revealed monstrous three-toed tracks scoring the sands. Panic took hold until Sarah's examination calmed nerves; tracks led not to shore but parallel within surf, as if their maker walked submerged yet on land.

Still, an omen of the profound changes reshaping the blue wilderness had been delivered. Fragments' power was inexorably warping all life it touched in alien and threatening ways.

As watch expanded further, would more twisted forms be uncovered? And could the Presence enhancing mutations be contacted, its goals understood and cooperative relations found before evolutions ran entirely out of humanity's control? These fears weighed heavy as the sun rose on another day of uncertain watch, and evolution's uncharted course accelerated into unknown deeps.

Evidence of Evolution

Weeks passed with no further sightings, yet an air of unease pervaded the village. Then one morn, cries rang out from the northern bluffs - something immense was moving through the surf.

Sarah gathered her supplies and raced to join the crowd assembling at the cliff's edge. Gasps arose as, cresting waves, a colossal serpentine form emerged, its armored hide glistening unnaturlly in the dawn light.

"Like nothing in God's creation," breathed Thomas. Before speculation could mount, the creature sounded, vanishing into the deep. But its brief appearance only deepened fears - what twisted forms might further patrols uncover?

That night, Sarah reviewed samples collected from prior finds. Under her microscope, fibrous tissues had reorganized into unfamiliar geometries.

"The fragments accelerate evolution far beyond normal bounds," she told the elders. "Each new form shows progressively more radical changes, as if working towards some strange new paradigm of life."

As debate grew around Sarah's grim findings, shouts rang out - lights had been spotted moving through the forest under the waxing moon.

Grabbing torches, the group hurried into the woods. There, flickering between the oaks, floated myriad glowing orbs, pulsing with an eerie bioluminescence.

"Fairy lights - but their behavior is abnormal," whispered Aoife. Yet as they watched, one orb drifted towards a pool. There, its luminance intensified, rousing shining responses from the depths before all disappeared beneath the murk.

Ripping divers for samples, what surfaces defied rational thought: fibrous shells surrounding luminescent tissues, more complex than any known organism.

Wordless, Sarah conveyed her prize to her lab. Under study, impossibilities were revealed - bioluminescent cells clustered like miniature constellations, communicating through light and pattern in ways beyond nature's known bounds.

A profane intelligence seemed to glimmer behind these mutations' intricate designs. But to what ends was such radical evolution progressing, and how long until transformations spilled from water and wood to engulf all lands?

Days passed as Sarah studied the bizarre specimens gleaned from forest and sea. Their anomalous structures challenged all known principles of biology.

At last, she convened the village. "Through fragments' enhancement, evolution accelerates towards terra incognita. Each new form grows progressively more sophisticated and alien."

Murmurs arose until Father Michael spoke. "Yet within God's creation, all serves purpose. Perhaps cooperation may be found if we understand evolution's design."

Thomas agreed. "Contact with the entity enhancing mutations could reveal intent and whether balance may be preserved."

It was decided small groups would further patrol woods and coast, documenting changes while seeking communication. Yet as scouting began anew, would signs of mutation shake even the hardiest faith in a rational order to the natural world?

Days passed uneventfully. Then in the forest's deepest glade, impossible tracks were found - three-pronged and immense, far too large to belong to any terrestrial creature. All knew something monstrous now prowled the wildwood under cover of dark.

Dread gripped the village as word spread of the unnatural tracks. That night, extra sentries were posted in the woods, torches at the ready.

For hours an eerie calm prevailed. Then shortly past midnight, cries rent the air - from the eastern fringe came the sounds of crashing undergrowth and snapping branches.

Racing towards the commotion, the patrol arrived to a chilling scene - one of their number lay dead, torn apart by savage claws. Nearby, glowing eyes peered from the shadows, far larger than any natural predator's.

Before anyone could react, the creature lunged with impossible speed, snatching another sentry in its jaws. Its armored hide glinted strangely as it dragged its prey into the gloom.

The remaining men fled in terror, the forest's silence closing around their retreat. All now knew some twisted new hunter had claimed the wildwood as its domain.

As dawn's light fell over the village, a somber Sarah addressed the traumatized folk. "Through fragments' enhancement, evolution progresses towards alien shores beyond reckoning. We must find way to contact the entity driving these changes, lest all lands be overrun by forms antithetical to life as we know it..."

But how long until even dialogue could no longer stem the tide of uncanny mutations reshaping the very fabric of the natural world?

A Shifting Ally

In the aftermath of the forest attack, fear gripped the village. Sarah knew contact with the entity enhancing mutations was now urgent if worse changes were to be averted.

That night, under a waxing moon, she ventured alone to the cliffs overlooking the restless sea. There she enacted rites handed down through generations, calling on primal forces beyond mortal ken.

As incense smoke drifted on the surf-borne breeze, luminescence gathered far below. Rising from the depths approached a vast, amorphous form, its flesh glimmering with an unearthly radiance.

A voice like the roar of deep currents echoed in Sarah's mind. "Your kind interests me, land dwellers. But changes wrought shall not be undone."

Remaining calm, Sarah replied, "Only to ensure balance is our intent. If we understand evolution's design, perhaps cooperation can be found."

The entity pulsed in thought. "Balance shifts as the world changes. Adapt or be left behind. But know all life is connected - harm one, harm all. Your kind and mine may learn from each other, if prepared for wild tides ahead."

Hope arose in Sarah's heart at the prospect of alliance. But could understanding be found before transformations escaped all control?

Sarah returned to the village as dawn broke, sharing hopeful news of first contact. Yet doubts remained - how prove the entity's intent was cooperation not domination?

That evening, she ventured again to the cliffs. Below, the radiant presence awaited. "Your kind enhances changes beyond nature's ordinary way. To what purpose drives this radical evolution?" Sarah asked.

The entity's song echoed in her mind. "All exists in flux. What you call evolution is simply flow of existence into new forms. My kind quickens this flow so all may adapt to a shifting world."

"But these changes threaten to overwhelm us," Sarah replied. "How ensure transformations don't escape all order and reason?"

The presence pulsed in thought. "A bridge between our kinds is needed. One attuned to both land and sea may mediate the flow, steer changes within... cooperation's bounds."

Sarah realized what was being proposed. But could such a union be possible, or safe? And what changes might it wreak upon her own being? Still, if it ensured balance, the risk seemed one that must be taken.

That night, Sarah explained the entity's proposal to the village elders. Thomas voiced gravest doubts.

"To merge land and sea so intimately? 'Tis madness, an affront to God's order."

Father Michael replied cautiously. "Yet if balances our peril, is such a union not something divine Providence may permit?"

After long debate, it was decided Sarah alone could decide what was asked of her. If any could be trusted to mediate such a boundary-crossing, it was their wise leader.

That evening, she returned to the cliffs. The radiant presence emerged, pulsing expectantly. Sarah steeled her nerve. "I understand what is proposed. To ensure harmony between your kind and mine, I am willing to serve as bridge."

The entity radiated approval. It slowly merged its luminous flesh with Sarah's, suffusing her with its alien song. Pain like the crushing deeps overcame her...

When Sarah woke at dawn, she had been changed. Gills adorned her neck while fins raced along her arms. Had the union worked, or dammed her between two worlds?

Sarah returned uncertainly to the village. Gasps arose at her alien yet stunning transformation. Thomas voiced gravest fears.

"The heathen entity has claim'd your soul! You can no longer dwell among God-fearing folk."

Before hostility could rise, Father Michael interjected. "Though changed in form, is she not still our beloved leader? Judge not by outward signs alone."

Sarah spoke. "Within I remain as I ever was. My form is but a bridge 'tween living kinds. Through cooperation, worse changes may yet be stayed."

Testing her gifts, she dove effortlessly into the surf. From ocean depths her song rang clear in villagers' minds: "All is well! My union with the entity has wrought strange powers, but also understanding 'tween our peoples. Together may we steer evolution's flow to shores where harmony holds sway..."

Hope was rekindled that terrible changes reshaping land and sea could indeed be navigated through unity, not division. Sarah's metamorphosis, while unnatural, proved that between seeming opposites, compassion might blossom in mankind's darkest hour. And with open hands and hearts, even barriers 'tween mortal and immortal could be crossed for life's sake. This, all took as an omen of promise amid perilous tides.

Shadows in the Surf

Weeks passed as Sarah mediated between village and sea. Through her guidance, further monstrous changes were steered away from settlements onto open waters. Yet unease lingered that not all mutations served harmony.

One moonlit night, Sarah ventured alone to the cliffs. Below, the radiant presence of her ally emerged from the surf.

"Not all share our goal of balance," its song echoed in her mind. "Dark currents now flow through the deep, twisting evolution toward fell designs."

Sarah felt concern. "What new threats have emerged? How can we counter such shadows on the tide?"

The entity pulsed uncertainly. "An ancient malice has stirred, seeking to sow chaos through twisted life. Its spawns now haunt offshore reefs under cover of night..."

Before more could be said, shrieks rang out across the bay. From inky waters rose misshapen forms, backlit by the gibbous moon. Their alien silhouettes sent dread through Sarah's soul.

The twisted shapes descended upon a fishing boat caught out past dusk. Snatching up sailors in clawed limbs, they dragged their terrified prey beneath the waves.

Sarah knew she must act to save the others. Diving from the cliffs, her new form carried her with imposible speed through the moonlit sea.

Arriving at the boat, three of the shadowy creatures yet remained, rending the hull. With a cry, Sarah lunged, tackling one overboard. They grappled as her allies surfaced, driving off the last assailants with sonic blasts.

Exhausted, Sarah emerged victorious from the surf, dragging the fallen foe behind. Upon the sands its misshapen form was revealed: a horrid fusion of shark and octopus, with too many eyes and teeth.

The villagers drew back in horror and prayer. But Sarah sensed this was but a harbinger of greater evils awakening in the deep...

She resolved to learn the source of darkness and counter its perversions, whatever nightmares lay beyond the reef. For too long had balance hung by a thread as evolution spiraled into the abyss.

Sarah brought the captured abomination to her lab for study. Under her microscope, its cells seethed with an unnatural vitality, mutating before her eyes.

She conveyed her findings to the village elders. "A fell intelligence is enhancing mutations beyond the entity's designs. We must determine its nature and intentions, lest the seas be overrun by twisted life."

hat night, accompanied by her radiant allies, Sarah dove deep along the reefs. There, lurking in crevices, she sensed an ancient malice watching through lidless eyes.

A voice like the shriek of tortured souls echoed in her mind. "None may stand against the coming chaos. All shall be remade in my image through blasphemous evolution."

Steeling her resolve, Sarah replied, "Only balance ensures life's continuity. Your perversions shall not stand."

Enraged, an immense, kraken-like form emerged from the abyss. Its countless writhing limbs seized Sarah as her allies attacked in defense. But would their powers prove equal to this primeval evil?

As the battle raged, Sarah was dragged ever deeper into frigid blackness. She knew unless freed, all hope to stem the rising shadows might be lost.

In the village, all awaited word of Sarah with mounting fear. Then, in the dead of night, her cry rang out across the surf.

Racing to the coast, they found her washed ashore, gravely wounded but alive. Gathering around, Father Michael began prayers to deliver her soul.

As dawn broke, Sarah stirred, eyes glowing with an unearthly light. She struggled to speak, conveying all that had transpired in the abyss.

There, in the deepest fathoms, she had faced the fell entity enhancing chaos through twisted evolution. Though near death, with her allies' aid she had banished the ancient evil back into the eternal night.

ut its corruption had seeped into her vein, awakening strange new powers behind her eyes. Though her body now served harmony between living kinds, her soul had glimpsed vistas of such cosmic chaos that sanity hung by a thread...

As she was brought back to health, all realized darker forces now lurked below the waves' calm surface. But with Sarah's gifted guidance, perhaps a harmony could yet be found between mankind and the mutable tides of life, steering evolution's flow to shores where reason and compassion held sway. This, all took as hope amid the shadows of an ever-changing world.

***

Chapter 05

RISING RISKS BELOW

Pack Mentality

With the ancient evil banished, an uneasy peace fell upon the coast. But Sarah sensed darker changes brewing in the depths.

One moonlit night, she ventured beneath the waves, scouting the reefs. There, she came upon a grisly scene - a great white lay slain, its flank torn open. Nearby, a pack of monstrous sharks circled, glowing eyes watching her hungrily.

She recognized their twisted forms - enhanced with alien traits. The fell entity's corruption yet lingered in these waters, warping evolution's flow.

As the sharks closed in to attack, her radiant allies surfaced and drove them off with sonic blasts. But Sarah feared it was but a glimpse of the wild mutations taking hold in the deep...

Returning to the village, she shared her grim discovery. Thomas voiced fears the sea would soon run red with blood. But Father Michael counselled hope - "Where chaos strikes, order may yet blossom through unity."

Sarah knew they must find way to steer these warped predators back to the path of harmony. If left unchecked, the sharks' twisted pack mentality may lead them to view all surface life as prey...

That night, Sarah ventured again to the reef, hoping to make contact. Sure enough, the shark pack soon circled, eyes glinting with feral hunger.

Projecting calm yet commanding thoughts, Sarah called out: "Brothers of the deep, why do you stray from balance's way? Twist evolution no further, lest you damn both your kind and mine."

One shark broke from the others, approaching cautiously. Its warped voice echoed in her mind. "The deep currents twist our nature, stoking ancient hungers. We know not why, only that to kill is in our blood."

"All life is connected," Sarah replied. "Your violence harms the whole of ocean and shore. Let me guide you back to the harmony between predators and prey."

The shark pulsed, considering. Its pack moved restlessly, thirsting for carnage. Finally it answered, "We will follow, if you prove stronger than the tides of madness within. But steer us wrongly, land dweller, and your flesh will feed our wrath."

Sarah had gambled all on cooperation. Now she could only hope compassion's power proved greater than the corruption's grip...Over coming nights, Sarah led the shark pack on hunting expeditions, teaching them to select only the old or sick for prey. Through patience and understanding, she slowly guided their twisted instincts back towards balance.

But one shark resisted, growing ever more vicious. Its eyes blazed with an unnatural fury as it challenged Sarah's leadership.

A vicious fight ensued between the two, but Sarah's allies came to her aid, driving the rogue shark off wounded. She knew, however, that not all mutations could be steered so easily.

Returning to the village, Sarah shared her progress - and concerns. "One shark has fallen fully to corruption's sway. We must find a way to isolate such lost souls, lest their madness spread through the pack."

Thomas voiced fears any compromise would endanger villagers. But Father Michael said "Desperate times call for bold acts of faith. Perhaps even the most warped may find redemption, in time, through compassion's power."

Sarah agreed - with care and vigilance, even fell mutations need not doom both man and beast. She resolved to build a secluded lagoon, allowing the pack solace while containing threats...if the rogue shark could be captured alive.

That night, a fierce storm raged over the bay. Sarah braved the torrential rains to check on the shark pack's cove.

To her horror, she found the rogue shark attacking its packmates under cover of the storm. Its eyes blazed with a hellish light as it ravaged all in its path.

Sarah knew she must stop the maddened beast before it butchered the entire pack. Charging into the fray, she grappled with the shark as lightning lit the roiling waves.

After a brutal struggle, she managed to subdue and bind the shark, dragging it from the cove as the others looked on in shock. The storm finally passed as dawn broke over a calm sea.

Sarah had saved the pack, but the rogue shark now thrashed furiously in her grasp, a slave to the corruption within. She resolved to keep it contained, hoping in time even such a warped soul might find peace.

As for the pack, under Sarah's watch they continued healing, suggesting even vast changes in nature need not doom what connections remain. This brought hope that through compassion's power, harmony might yet blossom amid rising tides of chaos.

Seeking Solutions

With the rogue shark contained, Sarah turned her focus to understanding the corruption's spread. In her lab, she studied cells from the maddened beast, hoping to discern how the fell entity's influence worked.

Night and day she toiled, aided by her allies' insights. Slowly, patterns emerged - the corruption seemed to hijack natural mutations, warping them towards violence and decay. But its exact mechanism eluded her...

Returning exhausted to the village, Sarah shared her findings. Thomas voiced fears no solution could be found. But Father Michael said "Where there is life, there is hope. Have faith that through cooperation, an answer may yet come to light."

That night, as Sarah rested, her ally's song echoed in her dreams - "Sister of the sea and shore, do not lose hope. In nature's balance lies the key...seek answers where land meets wave..."

The next dawn, Sarah walked the beach, contemplating the entity's words. And there, amid the tideline's bounty, she spotted glistening cells with properties unlike any she'd seen.

Sarah collected samples of the strange cells under her microscope. To her amazement, they seemed able to absorb mutagens without corruption, breaking them down into harmless compounds.

Could these tideline organisms hold the key to cleansing twisted mutations? She shared her findings with the village, renewing their hope. But questions remained - how could such properties be harnessed?

That night, her ally sang again - "Sister, you have found part of the solution's form. Now seek its function - observe where waves meet shore each day and night, and balance's harmony you may come to see."

The next dawn, Sarah rushed to the coast, watching intently. As tides ebbed and flowed, she realized - the organisms thrived by breaking down toxins from both land and sea, maintaining balance between the two.

Rushing back excitedly, she told the elders - "These tideline dwellers cleanse impurities through cooperation as land and sea interact daily. We must apply this principle to the corrupted!"

Father Michael smiled - "Unity and balance, it seems, hold the key even in nature's darkest hours. Now comes the hard part - finding safe way to deploy this gift against the corruption below..."

Sarah set to work cultivating the cleansing organisms in her lab, studying how their properties functioned. After many trials, she found a way to concentrate their mutagen-absorbing cells into a potent yet stable solution.

The next step was testing it on corrupted samples. To her elation, the solution broke down the mutations as predicted, restoring the cells to healthy balance. Hope surged that at last they had found an answer.

But questions remained - how to deliver the cure amid the deep's pressures? And would the corrupted accept help, or react with violence?

Sarah knew the rogue shark in containment must be the first subject. If it could be cured without harm, all else may follow. But attempting treatment risked unleashing its fury.

After long discussion, the elders agreed the risk was worth taking, to stem chaos below. That night, Sarah and her allies ventured to the lagoon under cover of darkness, hoping the corrupted one might find redemption through balance restored.

In the lagoon, the rogue shark thrashed furiously against its bonds. Sarah injected the cure solution into its bloodstream, then stood back with her allies, praying it would take hold before the shark broke free.

For moments that seemed an eternity, nothing happened. Then slowly, the unnatural light faded from the shark's eyes, which regained a semblance of sanity. Its struggles weakened as corruption's grip loosened.

Sarah approached cautiously, sending soothing thoughts. To her joy, the shark now recognized her as guide, not foe. With balance restored, its nature reverted from madness to its proper course.

She had succeeded - where chaos struck, through cooperation and faith, order could blossom anew. Sarah resolved to spread the cure throughout the tainted waters, knowing now that even in corruption's darkest reign, redemption remained possible through compassion's power.

As for the healed shark, she set it free to rejoin its pack, their bond now one of trust instead of forced rule. From this success, hope surged that the rising risks below might yet be stemmed, harmony's way found even amid vast changes wrought by time.

Shelter from the Storm

Heartened by success against the corruption, Sarah began spreading the cure solution throughout the tainted waters. Her allies aided, carefully dosing infected zones.

Within days, reports came of warped sharks and fish regaining balance. Hope soared that order may prevail where chaos struck. But a greater threat loomed on the horizon...

One stormy night, Thomas rushed to Sarah's lab with dire news - a vast cyclone approached, its winds threatening to tear apart their village. She knew shelters must be made to withstand the coming onslaught.

Racing to the elders, Sarah said "The tideline dwellers withstood ocean's wrath for eons. Let us build shelters mimicking their flexible, anchored forms to ride out the storm."

All worked through that night and the next day, weaving shelters from woven sea grasses anchored with stone. As evening fell, the cyclone struck with fury, howling winds and rains lashing the coast. But the shelters held strong.

As the storm raged, Sarah could only pray their efforts proved enough, and that the corruption's spread had been curbed below before the maelstrom hit.

The cyclone battered the coast through the night, waves crashing violently against the shore. Inside their shelter, Sarah and the villagers huddled anxiously, praying the defenses would hold.

Just after midnight, when hope seemed lost, the howling winds began to die down. Cautiously, Sarah peered outside to find the storm had passed, the shelters intact against the onslaught. Cheers of relief rose up within.

Come dawn, they ventured out to survey the damage. Miraculously, though debris was strewn along the beach, the village remained standing strong. Sarah thanked the elders for their resilience and cooperation in the face of disaster.

But greater worries lingered - had the corruption withstood the maelstrom below? Sarah dove beneath the waves, sending out calls which her allies relayed through the depths. To her joy, responses echoed back - the tainted waters had endured.

Returning ashore, she shared the good news. Father Michael smiled "Through unity and care for one another, even vast forces of nature can be weathered. Now comes the work of rebuilding what this storm washed away."

Hope rekindled, the villagers set to clearing debris and mending damages and nets. Though greater storms may come, their community had proven strong through compassion for all - humans and creatures alike.

In the days that followed the storm, Sarah continued monitoring the waters for signs of the corruption. To her relief, the cure seemed to be taking hold throughout the infected zones.

Mutated fish regained normal colorings and behaviors as balance was restored. Even the great white she had found slain bore no traces of enhancement. It seemed the maelstrom had helped purge remaining toxins.

Heartened, Sarah shared her findings with the villagers. But Thomas voiced new concerns - "With the tides shifting sandbars and reefs, old fishing routes may now be blocked. We must map changes to survive the seasons ahead."

The elders agreed and so, over many nights, Sarah led expeditions to chart alterations to the coastline and seafloor. Slowly, a new map of the realm emerged.

One area in particular now hosted thriving new coral growth. Bioluminescent plankton flickered over sandy flats. It seemed from chaos, nature was bringing forth renewal...

They named this bountiful region the Garden of Hope, a symbol that through resilience and care, even vast upheavals could seed positive change. United, people and sea would weather all storms to come.

With the new map complete, Sarah felt hopeful the village could thrive amid the changes. But one question lingered - what of the entity that had corrupted the deep?

That night, her ally sang to her: "Sister, you have triumphed over threats both above and below. But vigilance must remain, for where life exists, so too can chaos stir. Keep watch, and guide all toward harmony's way."

Reassured, Sarah resolved to continue monitoring the waters for any resurgence of the corruption. Through cooperation with humans and sea creatures alike, she knew balance could be maintained even in the face of unknown future threats.

Looking out over the newly mapped coast, now teeming with renewed life thanks to the storms' passage, Sarah felt pride in all they had accomplished through compassion and resilience of spirit. Though greater challenges may come, their community had proven its strength.

With care and understanding between all people and beings, harmony could blossom amid even the wildest changes wrought by the waves of time. This gave her hope that through their unity, any threat to the balance of ocean or shore might yet be overcome.

What Lies Beneath

With the waters cleansed and mapped anew, the village entered a period of rebuilding and renewal. But Sarah sensed another threat lurked in the deep, and resolved to discover its nature.

She dove below once more, sending out calls that echoed through the reefs. After several nights, a response came - from beyond the mapped borders lay mysterious ruins, their origins unknown.

Sarah shared her finding with the elders. Thomas was wary, but Father Michael said "All knowledge helps us understand nature's balance. With care and cooperation, even secrets of the deep may be illuminated."

The next night, Sarah led an expedition beyond the mapped borders, following the response calls. As they dove deeper into uncharted waters, strange formations emerged from the murk ahead.

Great stone pillars stretched upwards, adorned with carvings unfamiliar. Schools of fish flickered around archways leading into darkness. What ancient civilization had dwelt here, and what had become of it?

Its mysteries only deepened Sarah's resolve to uncover the truth of what lay beneath the waves.

Sarah signaled for the others to follow cautiously as she swam into the archway, sending out echolocation clicks. Shadowy structures loomed ahead, covered in coral and strange markings.

Small bioluminescent creatures flickered to light their way, as if welcoming the visitors. Sarah was filled with wonder at discovering a place untouched by humans for who knew how long.

Rounding a corner, they entered a vast central chamber. More pillars stretched upward into the gloom, adorned with carved figures of sea creatures. In the center lay a stone dais bearing an ornate symbol.

Sarah recognized it as similar to those seen on the corrupted shark. Could this ancient place somehow be connected to the fell influence? She knew they must investigate further.

As the group prepared to search the area, sudden movement caught their eyes. From the shadows emerged sleek, shark-like figures, watching them with an eerie, unearthly glow.

Sarah and the others froze, eyeing the strange sharks cautiously. Their glow was like nothing natural, with an otherworldly hue.

Seeking to avoid conflict, Sarah sent soothing thoughts and images of cooperation. To her relief, the sharks' glow softened as if recognizing she meant no harm. They circled slowly, almost...guiding.

Taking this as a sign of acceptance, Sarah bowed respectfully to the sharks. A flickering image formed in her mind - an invitation to follow. Exchanging looks, the group did so cautiously.

The sharks led them through twisting tunnels lined with more carvings, the walls emitting their own soft radiance. Snatches of images flashed in Sarah's thoughts - of a great civilization that had thrived here long ago in harmony.

Finally, they arrived at a vast chamber. At its heart stood three towering pillars glowing with an energy like the sharks'. Sarah realized - these ruins held mysteries that could help explain the corruption's source.

Sarah approached the pillars cautiously, sensing their power. As she neared, words echoed in her mind - an ancient language sharing the history of this place.

These ruins were a sanctuary for a long-lost people who lived in balance with sea and shore. But a darkness had arisen, corrupting some and driving the civilization into the deeps. Only these guardian sharks remained.

Now Sarah understood - the corruption they had faced was no random mutation, but a fell influence that had destroyed this ancient world. And its source still lurked in the depths, awaiting a chance to spread chaos once more.

As the words faded, the sharks' glow intensified, showing images of fighting back the darkness through cooperation and compassion. Sarah vowed to do just that, and share what she learned with the villagers.

Though a new, deeper threat had been revealed, she felt hope - by understanding the past and working together with all beings, even such a force of chaos could be opposed. The future, as ever, would be written by how people and ocean chose to stand as one.

***

Chapter 06

CITY OF CREATURES

A Surprising Structure

With the mysteries of the ancient ruins revealed, Sarah felt both wonder and concern about the lingering darkness below. She knew they must learn more to protect their village.

One night, her ally sang of a strange sighting far out to sea - a vast structure emerging from the depths, unlike any reef or wreckage. Sarah gathered the elders, sharing this new discovery.

"We must investigate," she urged. "Knowledge of such a place could aid our understanding of both the ocean's secrets and how to safeguard our home." The elders agreed, and so Sarah led an expedition beyond their mapped waters.

After many nights of diving ever deeper, a great form took shape in the murk ahead. Massive stone spires stretched upwards from ocean floor. Schools of fish fluttered between archways of a long-submerged city.

Cautiously, Sarah signaled the others to follow her into the alien streets. Bioluminescent plankton flickered to light their way past strange carved figures. What mystery lay within this watery metropolis so far from shore?

Rounding a corner, the group arrived in a vast central square. More towering pillars stretched upwards, their tops fading into the gloom.

Weaving between the formations were sleek shapes - but not sharks. As the creatures drew near, Sarah saw they were like no fish before.

Smooth skin stretched over lithe, mammalian forms. Glowing eyes peered from intelligent faces, observing the visitors with curiosity. Telepathic images flickered across Sarah's mind - welcome, and invitation to follow.

Exchanging glances, Sarah and the others cautiously trailed the strange sea mammals through winding alleyways. Snatches of shared history showed a oneness with the ocean that put villagers' dependence to shame.

More wonders appeared - gardens of corals and kelp, homes woven from maritime plants. Schools of smaller cetaceans fluttered past. At last the mammals arrived at a grand building, guiding the group inside.

Within shone the greatest marvel yet - a sphere of swirling energy, illuminating mysterious symbols across towering walls. Sarah sensed this place held answers about guardians of the deep.

Entering the great hall, Sarah gazed in awe at the glowing sphere. Telepathic images from the sea mammals told of its purpose - a well of natural energy harnessing oceanic powers, and focal point for their advanced civilization.

All turned as soft singing echoed. From a corridor emerged elders of the pod, their song welcoming. Bowing respectfully, Sarah sent greetings and asked to learn more of this place.

The elders' song replied of guarding the ocean realm since ancient times, in balance with all within it. But darker forces still stirred below, and threats arose that even these guardians struggled to counter.

Sarah realized the corruption they faced must be one such threat. She shared all that had befallen the surface - the storms, mutations, ruins discovered. The elders listened gravely, images flashing of similar shadows from eras long past.

As their song ended, one elder approached. "Together perhaps a solution may be found, but dangers lie ahead we cannot foresee. Vigilance and unity are needed now more than ever before."

Resolved, Sarah vowed to forge a strong alliance between ocean guardians and surface folk, to stand against the encroaching darkness.

The elder's words gave Sarah hope - with the wisdom and power of the ocean guardians aiding the villagers, surely any resurgence of corruption could be resisted. She knew maintaining balance would require open cooperation across all domains of sea and shore.

As the pod shared more of their history and home, Sarah felt awe and gratitude for this glimpse into a world so different yet interconnected with her own. Through song and image, bonds of trust and understanding were strengthening between the once-separate peoples.

By the time Sarah and the others began their journey back towards the surface once more, a new chapter of partnership had begun. With open exchange of knowledge and vigilance and compassion to guide them, Sarah felt their communities were now allied as never before against the deeper threats lurking the deep.

Though darker days may yet come, the discovery of the pod and their metropolis gave Sarah faith that by standing together with all beings of the ocean, any challenge to the harmony of wave and world could be met.

Creatures Cooperating

Word of the ocean guardians' city spread quickly through Sarah's village. All were eager to learn from their new allies, and many volunteered to make the journey beneath the waves.

Sarah led another expedition, this time with many villagers in tow. The pod welcomed them into their grand halls once more. Through song and thought, introductions were made between surface folk and cetaceans.

The pod elder spoke: "Our peoples must work as one if threats are to be countered. Let cooperation begin here - share your skills, and we ours."

A young dolphin swam up. "I will guide the surface swimmers through our home and teach reef navigation. Follow me!" Laughter rang as they set off.

Elsewhere, villagers mingled with pod craftsfolk. Kelp weavers showed techniques for plaiting sturdy ropes. Coral sculptors demonstrated carving tools from seashells.

An idea sparked in Sarah - "Your arts could benefit the village! We'll trade wood carvings and woven baskets for your works." The pod agreed eagerly.

s bonds of mutual understanding grew, Sarah hoped it marked a turning point - from separate communities to one interwoven family across all domains of sea and shore.

The days passed swiftly as cooperation blossomed. Villagers learned reef navigation, signaling, and hunting techniques from the pod. In turn, cetaceans gained skills like net-mending, boat-building, and shore ecology.

ne morning, a young orca swam to Sarah. "My pod-kin sense a storm brewing far out. Its power seems...wrong, twisted. We must investigate together."

Worry crept over Sarah but she agreed - facing threats was why their alliance formed. She gathered a crew of villagers and pod members, then followed the orcas beyond familiar waters.

As they swam, dark clouds loomed ahead. Lightning flashed within the mass, but it lacked the rhythm of nature. Sarah sensed the same fell influence behind it.

Reaching the storm's edge, the waters churned with strange energy. Among the waves, villagers and cetaceans spotted flashes of twisted shapes - corals fused with eels, crabs with serpents' tails. All were corrupted, attacking any creatures near.

Sarah steeled herself. This was why understanding between peoples must grow - so united, none would stand alone against such darkness. She signaled for a coordinated assault, to end the mutants' threat without further harm.

The villagers and pod members worked seamlessly together. Using nets, ropes and natural weapons, they subdued the corrupted creatures with minimal injury. Sarah's heart swelled seeing such cooperation in action.

Yet the storm's core raged on, fed by some deeper evil. As they debated their next move, a colossal shadow loomed beneath. From the murk emerged a kraken of impossible size, its bulk twisted with growths. Mutated tentacles lashed out.

Sarah knew direct combat was futile. She called for evasive maneuvers while transmitting calm and understanding. To her relief, many pod elders responded, surrounding the beast with soothing songs.

Slowly its rage subsided as the elders' harmony took hold. Its form began shrinking as the corruption receded. When at last it was normal in size, the kraken retreated peacefully into the depths once more.

The storm faded without its dark fuel. Sarah smiled at her aquatic allies, proud of what they'd achieved through unity rather than force. But she wondered - what drove this twisted transformation, and how to fully purge the ocean of its foul influence?

With the corrupted creatures vanquished and the kraken restored to normal, the villagers and pod felt triumphant yet wary. They had witnessed firsthand how swiftly darkness could warp the natural order.

As they began the journey back, the pod elder spoke to Sarah telepathically. "This evil seeks to divide and corrupt all in its path. We must strengthen our alliance to stand against it."

Sarah agreed. "Together we can oppose such forces. Our peoples will work as one from this day onward."

Renewed in purpose, the two communities returned home. But Sarah remained determined to learn the source of the corruption, and free the ocean realm entirely. With the pod at her side and bonds of trust between all, she felt ready to face any threat.

From that day, the village and pod city were truly woven into one interdependent community across sea and shore. Through cooperation, balance would be maintained and darkness kept at bay. And so a new chapter of harmony between all ocean beings had only begun.

Teeming with Life

With the threat of the twisted storm subdued, a period of growth and learning followed for the combined communities. Villagers regularly visited the pod city to study reefs, hunt with their allies, and exchange crafts.

Sarah often accompanied them, marveling anew each time at the bustling metropolis beneath the waves. Schools of colorful fish fluttered between coral towers. Gigantic whale sharks drifted like living islands. Octopuses wove seamlessly through rock crevices.

One day, exploring with her dolphin friend Tui, Sarah noticed something strange. "The waters seem...thicker somehow. I can barely see beyond my outstretched hand!"

Tui laughed. "You're swimming through the zooplankton bloom! Billions have gathered to feed and breed."

As their eyes adjusted, a dazzling sight emerged. Tiny shrimp-like creatures clouded the water in a swirling, dancing mass. Fish and jellies drifted amid the swarm, feeding in the abundance.

"It's one of the ocean's great wonders," said Tui. "Each year the plankton return to continue the cycle of life. Come, let's swim among them!"

Sarah swam cautiously into the thick cloud of zooplankton, amazed by the sheer numbers that blotted out all other sights. Yet within the bloom, a world of micro activity was happening.

Small fish darted to and fro, snapping up plankton. Jellyfish pulsed gently along, their tentacles trailing to catch the tiny creatures. Looking closer, Sarah spotted miniature shrimp-like forms, some carrying egg sacs or larvae.

"There is so much life, even among the smallest of beings," she said to Tui in wonder.

Just then, a massive shadow passed overhead. Looking up, Sarah gasped to see a great blue whale filtering through the bloom, its cavernous mouth agape. As it fed, plankton streamed out in endless ribbons.

"The bloom supports the largest creatures too," chuckled Tui. "Come, let's swim with the whale!"

Gaining the whale's calm acceptance, Sarah and Tui darted around its gigantic form. Through the whale's massive filter-feeding, the very foundations of the ocean's food web were sustained. Sarah felt humbled by nature's intricate balances.

As Sarah and Tui swam with the feeding blue whale, she noticed other large creatures joining the feast. Schools of mobula rays fluttered their wing-like pectoral fins to stir the plankton cloud, while manta rays gracefully skimmed their wide mouths through.

Further out, she spotted the unmistakable dorsal fins of orcas patrolling the swarms, snatching fish that had gathered to feed on plankton. Their fluid movements spoke of effortless hunting skills.

Weaving between the giants was a kaleidoscope of smaller life - anglerfish displaying bioluminescent lures, cuttlefish displaying camouflage talents, octopuses stretching out seeking arms. At the edges of Sarah's vision, bioluminescent flashes hinted at creatures even her eyes could not discern.

She turned to Tui, eyes alight. "The whole ocean is a web, each strand supporting countless others. How lucky we are to witness such wonders!" Tui nodded, pleased to share this glimpse of the teeming deep with her friend.

Just then, a tremor passed through the waters. The plankton cloud pulsed and the great filter-feeders slowed, sensing a change. Sarah felt a familiar ominous presence stirring in the depths below.

As the tremor faded, an eerie calm fell over the plankton bloom. Sarah and Tui exchanged worried glances - some new threat was rising from the ocean depths.

Tui sang out a message, calling the pod guardians to gather. Within moments, elders and warriors arrived alongside the whales and rays. Through song and thought, Sarah shared all she had sensed.

The elders agreed - whatever disturbed the waters was likely another manifestation of the ancient corruption. But facing it would require prudence over haste.

It was decided lookouts would be posted to monitor changes, while the rest retreated to let the plankton bloom disperse naturally. With their food source scattering, filter feeders and foragers safely followed the tide.

Sarah promised to send word if the village observed any odd happenings as well. Though darkness loomed, the pod's swift, coordinated response gave her hope. Their growing alliance meant no threat could catch them unaware on either side of the boundary now.

As always, standing together gave the best chance of countering whatever new form the corruption might take. And so vigilance continued across all domains of the vast, teeming ocean.

Protecting the Community

In the days that followed, an air of watchfulness fell over both village and pod city. Lookouts scanned shore and sea for any signs of the corruption's return.

One morning, a dolphin sentry swam urgently to Sarah. "Footprints along the reef - larger than any normal predator. And something...twisted about the tracks."

Worry lines creased Sarah's brow. "Show me." She gathered a group to investigate, including warriors of both lands.

Following the dolphin through kelp forests, Sarah gasped at the monstrous tracks pressing into coral and sand. Bones and scales littered the trail - remnants of creatures torn apart with brutal force.

A pod elder sang gravely, "These marks carry the taint we've sensed before. Some new threat stalks our domains."

Sarah nodded. "We must find it, and end its threat, before it harms others. Split into teams - follow the trail, but stay alert and call for aid at any sign of danger."

So the search parties fanned out, keeping communication open as they tracked the fell presence through the reefs. What new form of corruption had come, and could their alliance stand against it?

As the search parties followed the ominous trail, an eerie silence fell over the reef. No playful dolphin pods or foraging fish broke the stillness.

Suddenly, a panicked call rang out - "It's here! By the kelp grove!" Sarah spun to see a hulking, misshapen form emerge from the swaying plants. From shark to something far worse it had been twisted, with extra jaws and limbs jutting at unnatural angles.

It charged the calling pod member, who evaded its lunge narrowly. Thinking fast, Sarah signaled the others to flank it from all sides. If they could subdue it without harm, they might learn its source.

As the creature raged and snapped, villagers and cetaceans worked together seamlessly. Nets and ropes ensnared its limbs while song and touch calmed its frenzy. Step by step it was overcome, until at last it lay still - but what nightmares writhed within its form?

A pod elder swam close, placing a flipper on its brow. As all watched anxiously, the elder sang a low, soothing note...and the corruption began receding from the captive beast. Soon, a normal if exhausted shark remained.

Their cooperation had prevailed once more. But how long before an even greater threat arose from the ocean's heart of darkness?

As the freed shark was safely released back into the wilds, Sarah turned to the pod elder. "Your skills grow ever more crucial. But this evil seems to spread; we must find its source and end it for good." The elder nodded gravely. "The corruption draws power from some primal place. I can use my gifts to track its essence back - but the journey will be long and perilous."

"You shall not go alone," Sarah replied. She knew facing the threat's heart required their combined strengths. That night, volunteers from both communities prepared for the voyage. Coral craftsfolk outfitted a sturdy boat, while pod artisans wove enchanted fabrics for protection. Healers stocked remedies from both realms.

At dawn, Sarah and the elder set out with a crew of villagers, dolphins, and orcas. Waves parted smoothly before the boat as they sailed beyond familiar coasts.

For days they followed the corruption's dark trail, encountering twisted aberrations that attacked sporadically. Each time, teamwork subdued the threats with minimal harm.

Yet as they pushed into black and hostile deeps, even the elder grew uneasy. What nightmares lay at the route's end, and could their alliance withstand it?

As the corrupted deeps pressed in, Sarah felt the crew's apprehension rising. Even the elder sang notes of disquiet now.

She called for a rest, hoping respite would lift their spirits. But as all took refreshment, the waters shuddered with an ominous rumble. A massive shadow loomed ahead, blocking their path.

Rising from the abyss was a colossal kraken, its bulk twisted with tumors and eyes burning with malice. With an unearthly shriek, it lashed out massive arms tipped with nightmarish claws.

Sarah knew direct combat meant doom. She called for evasive maneuvers while the elder sang a calming harmony, aided by pod choruses. Their combined gifts began to quell the beast's rage.

Yet more shadows were emerging all around, more aberrations crawling from the depths. Sarah realized this was the corruption's last defense - it had summoned all its twisted minions to protect its heart.

Grimly she rallied her allies. "Today we face the darkness once and for all. With unity and courage, none can stand against us! For the ocean, attack!"

Their coordinated assault prevailed through teamwork and trust. When at last only black waters remained, their long journey was over. But what nightmares still lay ahead?

***

Chapter 07

A DANGEROUS DISCOVERY
IN THE WRECKAGE

What's in the Wreckage

With the last of the corrupted creatures vanquished, Sarah and the pod elder swam deeper into the abyss. An ominous structure loomed ahead through the murk - a sunken vessel, long corroded by the depths.

"This holds the heart of the darkness," sang the elder. Sarah nodded grimly. They gathered their allies to explore the wreck.

Dolphin sonar swept the hulk as villagers lit magelights. Within, a maze of rusted passages twisted into the gloom. Strange growths encrusted the metal walls like tumors.

As they pushed forward, Sarah spotted movement. "There!" A twisted form fled - half fish, half something else. The elder confirmed its corrupted nature but said to let it flee for now. Tracing it would lead nowhere; they must find the source.

Deeper into the wreck they swam, detecting flickers of movement all around. Sarah shivered, feeling malign eyes watching from the darkness. What unnatural experiments had bred these monstrosities?

Rounding a corner, the crew halted in horror. A vast chamber held cages of twisted, suffering captives - results of some insanity's experiments. But what nightmares lay beyond?

The group approached the cage area cautiously. Inside the rusted bars, twisted semi-humanoid creatures thrashed and moaned.

"These poor souls," said Sarah softly. "Can you help them, elder?"

The elder sang a calming note. Slowly the creatures stilled, recognizing a friend. As the elder soothed their tortured minds, their forms began to alter.

When at last the song ended, normal fish remained in the cages. The crew worked quickly to release them back to the sea.

"Whatever evil created this place has perverted the natural order," said the elder grimly. "We must stop it before more suffer such fates."

Nodding, Sarah led the way deeper. Around the next bend, a massive chamber opened before them, filled with strange machinery and glowing vials. Horrors floated lifeless within glass tubes.

At the center, a robed figure hunched over bubbling containers, muttering. It had not yet sensed their approach. Sarah signaled a pod warrior, who shot forward silently. With a quick strike, it subdued the figure.

Rolling it over, Sarah recoiled. Beneath the cowl was no normal face, but a nightmarish amalgam of animal and human features.

As the crew examined the unconscious figure, the elder sang a somber note. "This one's mind is far gone, consumed by its twisted experiments. Only madness remains."

Sarah shook her head sadly. "What drove it to such evil?" She noticed a leather journal among the machinery and opened it cautiously. Within were scribblings and diagrams too horrible to comprehend.

"It sought to meld lifeforms into new abominations," she said, horrified. "But its goals were madness. No good can come of violating nature's order so."

Just then, a tremor shook the wreck. Alarms blared from the machinery as lights flickered ominously. "We must flee, now!" cried Sarah. "This place is unstable after so long at the abyssal depths."

Gathering all the evidence they could carry, the crew fled the collapsing chamber. But as they swam from the groaning hulk, the twisted figure's eyes snapped open and burning hatred shone within its gaze.

It began chanting in an alien tongue that set Sarah's teeth on edge. The wreckage shuddered, then began dragging them all down into the endless dark. What new threat had they unleashed?

As the sunken wreck was pulled deeper by some malign force, Sarah realized they had to act fast to escape its pull.

"Elder, can your song counter that evil magic?" she asked urgently. The elder began singing a powerful harmony, its notes resonating with the ocean's life force.

radually the hulk's descent slowed, then stopped as the elder's magic battled the twisted one's spells. But they had to break free fully before the magic failed.

Thinking quickly, Sarah had villagers ignite smoke bombs while dolphins herded nearby sharks toward the wreck. As the sharks scented blood in the water and sighted the bombs' smoke, their predatory instincts took over.

With vicious bites and rakes, the sharks tore into the wreckage. Groaning metal gave way, and with a thunderous crash the hulk collapsed in on itself, trapping the screaming figure forever in the abyss.

As the last echoes faded, Sarah turned to her allies with a weary smile. "Thanks to our unity, the darkness is vanquished. Let us return home in peace."

With the corruption's end, a new era of cooperation had begun between all ocean dwellers. And so the intrepid crew sailed for home, their mission accomplished through courage, trust and teamwork against all odds.

A Grim Warning

Exhausted but triumphant, Sarah's crew returned to the village with tales of their harrowing quest. All rejoiced to hear the corruption was vanquished forever.

But examining the twisted journal more closely, a dark premonition gripped Sarah. She requested an urgent meeting of elders.

"This evil one raved of spreading its madness across all seas," she warned. "What if others seek to continue its work? We must be vigilant."

The elders agreed. One said gravely, "I will consult ancient records for any clues. And send out swimmers to nearby shores, in case other wrecks or labs went undiscovered."

Meanwhile, Sarah turned to the pod elder. "Your gifts allow communication across great distances. Please send out a warning - any who find strange vessels or creatures must report them at once."

The elder sang out a far-carrying message conveying Sarah's news and concerns. Now all ocean dwellers were on high alert for further signs of the corruption's lingering influence.

But little did they know the true threat had only just begun to stir, its vengeance now set upon all the seas.

A few days later, a panicked dolphin arrived with grim tidings. "Orcs attacking our northern pod - strange new weapons that burn and maim!"

Sarah's blood ran cold. This sounded all too similar to the corruption's twisted experiments. She gathered warriors at once.

"We must aid our allies with haste. Ready boats and provisions - it will be a long journey."

Soon they were racing northwards through rolling seas. As they sailed, Sarah questioned the dolphin further. "These orc raiders - did you detect any corruption's taint?"

The dolphin shuddered. "A darkness clung to them, though their forms were unchanged. And madness burned in their eyes..."

Dread coiled in Sarah's gut. It seemed the corruption's influence had found new hosts to spread its evil. She prayed they weren't too late to help the northern pod.

At last they reached the pod's waters, now stained red. Sarah gasped at the carnage - twisted orc creations rampaged through the pods. Some had gained horrific new abilities.

As Sarah and her allies took in the horrific scene, a pod elder swam up desperately. "You came...but I fear we're doomed. These orc beasts cannot be stopped like normal foes!"

Sarah steeled her nerves. "While life remains, there is hope. We've defeated this corruption before through unity. Where are the orcs attacking from?"

The elder pointed a trembling flipper towards a dark shape on the horizon - an enormous warship, its decks crawling with corrupted orcs wielding strange weapons that fired blasts of dark magic.

"We must board that vessel and cut off the source of their power," said Sarah. "Can your pod distract the beasts while we sneak aboard?"

The elder nodded and swam off to rally survivors. Meanwhile, Sarah's crew stealthily approached under cover of dusk. Scaling the warped hull, they peered over the rail to plan their attack.

But a sentry's gaze fell upon them, and with a guttural cry it raised the alarm. All chaos broke loose as orcs charged and twisted beasts surged towards the intruders. It was time for battle amid the corruption's dark heart.

As corrupted orcs and creatures swarmed the deck, Sarah knew this would be their toughest battle yet. But she had faith in her allies.

"For the pods, attack!" she cried, charging with villagers and cetaceans at her side. Their coordinated assault overwhelmed the first wave of foes.

Dodging blasts of dark magic, Sarah cut a path towards the command deck. There, a nightmarish general directed the forces, further mutated by the corruption's evil.

It turned with a snarl, unleashing a shockwave that sent Sarah flying. But the pod elder's song strengthened her, and she rolled to her feet unharmed.

With allies fighting valiantly behind her, Sarah engaged the general in a brutal duel. Its twisted abilities pushed her to her limit until, with a final roar, she severed its head.

All at once, the corrupted orcs froze - without their leader's will, the evil influence broke. As one, Sarah's forces subdued the last resistants.

he northern pods were avenged. With the warship destroyed, no further threat remained. Sarah smiled wearily as cheers rose up from both land and sea. Their unity had once more triumphed over darkness.

Though more evils may arise, as long as the oceans' peoples stood together, none could overcome them. Peace was restored to the waters, and Sarah's legend had only begun.

Plans in Motion

With the northern pods secured, Sarah returned home victorious once more. But troubling rumors had spread in her absence.

"More wrecks have been found - some holding living nightmares," warned the elders. Sarah's blood ran cold. It seemed the corruption was not so easily destroyed.

She requested the elders' counsel. "For now we fight isolated threats, but what if it spreads further? We must form a united defense."

The elders agreed. One said, "With pod cooperation, we can monitor all seas. The first sign of danger, a warning will sound."

But another shook her head. "Merely reacting helps little in the long run. We must root out the corruption at its source, not just symptoms."

A young orca spoke up: "My pod hunts far oceans. If given a description, we can search for the source's origin."

Sarah smiled. "A proactive solution. You seek the corruption's heart - we will prepare defenses here until you learn more." Plans were coming together.

The orca pod set off on their long journey, while Sarah focused on strengthening local defenses.

"Villagers, help the pods build an early warning network - signal spires that can alert all if danger is detected," she instructed.

Meanwhile, she had craftsmen forge special weapons imbued with the elder's magic. "These will help turn the tide if more twisted foes appear," the elder sang.

As the pods worked tirelessly, word came from scouting dolphins - a strange hulk had been sighted far west, near shores of a mysterious land. Could this be a new corruption stronghold?

Sarah gathered her most trusted crew. "We must investigate at once. If that wreck holds new evils, its secrets cannot be left undiscovered."

Under cover of night, they sailed stealthily towards the distant hulk. What nightmares might they find lurking within its rusted depths? And had they already set more plans in motion?

As Sarah's crew approached the hulk under cover of darkness, an eerie green glow emanated from within its corroded depths.

"Whatever lurks there has found a new power source," said Sarah grimly. "We must infiltrate silently and discover its nature."

Scaling the hull proved treacherous, but with teamwork they gained the deck. Strange growths pulsated with an unnatural light. Sarah touched one cautiously - it recoiled!

"The corruption has fused flesh and metal," she realized. "Be on guard, my friends."

Creeping through rusting passages, they detected shuffling and muttered curses ahead. Peering around a bend, Sarah gasped. Twisted humanoids in plate armor stood guard, experimenting on captives in glowing cages.

"Orcs! But mutated far beyond normal," she whispered. One guard turned, its gaze locking with Sarah's in an instant of pure malice.

It let loose an inhuman shriek, alerting the others. Sarah signaled retreat as armored footsteps thundered their way. They fled through twisting halls, the corrupted orcs in close pursuit.

With corrupted orcs closing in, Sarah led her crew in a desperate bid for escape. They turned a corner and found their path blocked by pulsating flesh walls.

"Through here, quickly!" cried Sarah, plunging her blade into the quivering mass. It split open with a sickening squelch, revealing an opening just large enough to slip through. One by one her allie darted inside, Sarah covering their retreat.

Just as the last crew member entered, the orcs rounded the corner. But with a thunderous boom, the flesh walls slammed shut before the monsters' very eyes.

Sarah and her friends found themselves in a dark, natural cave, the sounds of enraged orcs muffled behind the walls of corrupted flesh.

"We're safe for now," Sarah panted, "But we must hurry to warn the others. This evil has fused technology with the living in unnatural ways. If it spreads further..."

She didn't need to finish. They all knew the threat this corruption posed if not stopped. With haste they made their escape from the caverns, bearing grim news of what they'd witnessed for the elders to hear. The battle was far from over.

Dive into Danger

With the elders gathered, Sarah recounted their grim discovery. "This corruption has found new ways to spread - fusing the living and technological. If it isn't contained, who knows the horrors it could create?"

The elders conferred gravely. Finally, one spoke: "To understand our enemy, we must learn its secrets. A small group should infiltrate the wreck again, this time going deeper."

Sarah nodded. "I will lead a crew of our best warriors and researchers. With stealth and magic on our side, perhaps we can uncover its plans."

Preparations began at once. The elder imbued Sarah's team with protections, while craftsmen outfitted them with gear to withstand the depths.

Finally, under cover of night, Sarah's team returned to the hulk. Scaling its hull proved easier with their enhancements. They entered the flesh portals silently.

Within the pulsating corridors, Sarah's team proceeded cautiously. Strange shrieks and mechanical clanking echoed ahead.

Rounding a corner, they peered into a vast chamber. Corrupted orcs in armored suits worked on unholy experiments, fusing abominations with warped machinery.

A researcher whispered, "That armored beast - its flesh is becoming metal. And those orbs infect living tissue on contact!"

Sarah grimaced. "This corruption spreads its taint in new forms. We must find the source and sabotage their work."

Creeping past monstrosities, they entered tunnels leading deeper. The walls writhed with veins pulsing black ichor. A guard suddenly turned - it had sensed their magic!

As alarms blared and corrupted denizens gave chase, Sarah's team fled down twisting passages. One collapsed behind them, buying time.

A researcher cried, "Ahead - a massive organic core! It must be generating this evil!" Within a fleshy cavern, a nightmarish heart pulsated, surrounded by machinery extracting its power.

Sarah grinned. "We have found the source. Now to destroy it and halt this corruption's schemes!" How would they sabotage the living reactor before being overwhelmed.

The team crept toward the pulsating core, but a rumble alerted them - more corrupted guards approached.

"We must act fast," said Sarah. "Researchers, analyze how it works. Warriors, hold off the beasts."

As her allies engaged monstrosities at the tunnel's end, the researchers scanned the machinery. One cried "Aha! These tubes extract the core's essence. Sever them!"

Sarah and others drew their magic-imbued blades and hacked at writhing tubes. Black ichor sprayed as the core spasmed in pain. Its guardians shrieked and mutated further in their rage.

"It's working, keep cutting!" yelled Sarah over the din. More tubes parted under their assault. The core began to collapse in on itself.

The last tube was cut just as the first corrupted orcs charged in. With a horrible shriek, the core imploded - and a shockwave threw all back.

As silence fell, Sarah stood shakily. Where the core had been was now an empty, lifeless cavity. They had destroyed the source of this evil.

But as they fled the collapsing wreck, a troubling question lingered - where had this corruption originated, and what other horrors might still lie in wait?

With the hulk crumbling behind them, Sarah's team escaped through the flesh portals as the entire structure fell into the sea. They had severed the corruption's influence within these waters, but greater mysteries remained.

Returning to the pods, Sarah reported their findings. "This evil fused technology with life in blasphemous ways. But where did it come from originally?"

The elders pondered gravely. Finally, one spoke: "Legends tell of a sinister land across the eastern sea. Perhaps there we will find the true heart of this corruption."

Sarah nodded. "Then I will lead an expedition beyond our waters, to seek the source of this evil and understand its nature. With such knowledge, perhaps we can safeguard against future threats."

The pods agreed to support Sarah's quest. So with a small crew of warriors and scholars, she set sail into uncharted oceans. What nightmares might they find in the mysterious eastern land? And could any defense be prepared against an enemy of such cunning and malice?

Their voyage had uncovered more questions than answers. But Sarah was determined to learn the truth, and protect her home at all costs. Whatever lay ahead, she would face it with courage and unity. Thus began Sarah's most perilous mission yet into the very heart of darkness.

***

Chapter 08

FACE TO FACE IN THE DARK

Face to Face in the Dark

After weeks sailing uncharted seas, Sarah's crew spotted a foreboding shoreline looming through thick fog. Jagged mountains speared the mist, and an ominous glow emanated from within.

"This must be the eastern land," said Sarah grimly. "Prepare for anything - the corruption's heart may lie ahead."

They anchored on a black sand beach and disembarked warily. Twisted trees clawed the skies as Sarah's crew cut their way into the forest. Strange sounds echoed in the gloom.

A scout cried out - she had stumbled upon a monstrous pit. Peering over the edge, Sarah gasped. Twisted humanoids in cages screamed as snake-like machines drained their essence.

"The corruption has spread here as well," she realized. But before they could react, a guttural voice boomed: "Intruders! Seize them for the master!"

From the trees emerged corrupted orcs in spiked armor, eyes aglow with malice. Sarah drew her blade. "For our homes, attack!" A brutal battle was joined amid the mist.

The crew fought valiantly, but the corrupted orcs' twisted strength was immense. Sarah found herself surrounded, striking down foe after foe.

Suddenly, a massive orc chieftain appeared, twice the size of others. With a roar it swatted allies aside. Sarah braced for its charge, but a voice rang out:

"Hold, Ugrosh, these are no normal prey." Stepping from the mist was a nightmarish figure in spiked armor, eyes glowing red."Who are you?" demanded Sarah. The figure grinned. "I am Magnus the Defiler. This land and its people are mine to corrupt."

Magnus snapped his fingers. The orc Ugrosh backed down reluctantly. Sarah glared at the Defiler. "You're behind all this evil! Surrender or fight me yourself, coward."

Magnus laughed. "In time, podling. But first, you will tell me all - how you withstood my corruption before."

Sarah refused to yield. But with her crew overwhelmed, she had no choice but to follow Magnus into the mist.

Magnus led Sarah deep into the misty forest, surrounded on all sides by his corrupted minions. She glared at the Defiler but said nothing, determined not to show fear.

At last they emerged in a clearing, where rusted machines toiled day and night. Magnus gestured proudly. "Behold, the heart of my domain. Here I perfect the union of flesh and steel."

Sarah saw horrors beyond imagination - twisted beasts fused with machinery, pulsing with unholy power. But she remained stoic, asking "What is your goal, Defiler? Why corrupt all in your path?"

Magnus smiled cruelly. "Order through assimilation is all. Your pods' magic allowed resistance, but no longer. Soon all will merge as one under my command."

Sarah shook her head. "Free will cannot be stripped so easily. As long as one remains uncorrupted, your 'order' is doomed."

Magnus' eyes blazed. "We shall see about that, podling. For now, you will aid my experiments... by force if needed!"

What dark fate awaited Sarah at Magnus' hands? She must escape and spread word of this threat to all seas.

As Magnus' corrupted minions closed in, Sarah steeled herself for a final stand. But before they could seize her, a thunderous boom shook the forest.

From the mist emerged a pod of orcas, led by the elder. With magical song, he cast a shield around Sarah and her crew. "Your evil ends here, Defiler! Now face us and know justice!"

Magnus howled in rage. All around, pods from the distant seas appeared through portals, answering the elder's call to battle. As one, they charged the Defiler's forces.

Sarah joined the fight, battling at the elder's side. Though outnumbered, the pods' unity and magic evened the odds. Magnus raged as his machines were overrun.

At last only Magnus and Ugrosh remained. The elder challenged the Defiler to single combat, and a climactic duel commenced amid the mist and machines.

After a fierce struggle, the elder gained the upper hand. With a final blast of magic, Magnus was no more. His corruption died with him.

The forests grew light once more. Sarah embraced the elder, overjoyed at their victory. "The pods stood united against the darkness. No evil shall overcome our friendship again!"

And so the shadow of the Defiler was lifted from these lands. The pods had faced their greatest foe, and triumphed through courage and unity. Peace returned once more to the seas.

Battle Below

With Magnus defeated, Sarah and the elder led the pods in cleansing the corrupted forests. Machines were dismantled, and twisted creatures put out of their misery.

But as they worked, a scout burst into the clearing. "Elder, a storm brews - but something moves beneath the waves!"

The elder's eyes widened. "Magnus was not the only evil here. To the seas, quickly!"

As rain poured, the pods sped toward a churning maelstrom. Within its depths, a colossal shadow writhed.

Lightning flashed, revealing a nightmarish sight - a gargantuan squid, flesh fused with metal, tentacles crackling with energy.

Magnus' final creation," growled the elder. "We must stop it reaching the open ocean!"

The pods attacked as one, but beams from the squid's eyes sent many fleeing. Sarah cried "We need a new strategy - let me think!"

As the elder's pod was struck, Sarah got an idea. "Lure it towards the shore - I have a plan to ground the beast!"

The pods split into two groups. One drew the squid after them, narrowly dodging its attacks. The other lay in wait.

The squid took the bait, chasing the pods towards the shore. But as it neared the sandbar, Sarah cried "Now!"

The second pod group attacked from the flank, unleashing sonic blasts. The squid flailed in confusion, tentacles digging into the sandbar.

It was grounded but still deadly. The elder ordered a retreat as energy crackled in its eyes. But Sarah shouted "Watch its flesh - there must be a power source!"

Sure enough, a pulsing organ was visible where flesh met machine on its side. Sarah swam in close under cover of a pod. With a magic-enhanced blade, she sliced at the organ.

Black blood poured out as the squid shrieked, lashing about. But its movements slowed, energy fizzling out. Sarah cried "Together now - finish the beast!"

As one, the pods rammed and bit the flailing form. With a final shudder, the colossal fusion collapsed into the surf. The storm began to pass.

The elder nuzzled Sarah. "Your courage and wisdom saved us all. Magnus' evil is ended - thanks to you, podling."

The forests grew light once more. Sarah embraced the elder, overjoyed at their victory. "The pods stood united against the darkness. No evil shall overcome our friendship again!"

As the pods celebrated their victory, Sarah noticed a strange glow emanating from the fallen squid's remains. She called out to the elder.

"There is still something strange here. I'm going to investigate further."

Sarah dove down and swam through the murky water. As she approached the corpse, the glow intensified. Buried deep within its flesh was an unearthly object, pulsing with an unnatural light.

Sarah pulled at it with her teeth, trying to dislodge it. With a sickening squelch, it came free - but then the object began to hover in the water before her.

She cried out in alarm. The elder and the other pods swam swiftly to her aid. But before they could reach her, a beam of energy burst forth from the object, enveloping Sarah in its glow.

When the light faded, Sarah had vanished without a trace! The elder called out desperately, but there was no response from the murky depths.

What had happened to their brave podling? Where had the mysterious object taken her? As the pods searched frantically, a sense of foreboding fell over all present. Their victory over Magnus may have only been the beginning.

As night fell, the pods gathered in sorrow. Sarah was gone, vanished without a trace.

The elder spoke gravely: "This strange magic is beyond our understanding. But I know in my heart - Sarah's quest is not over."

One podling came forward nervously. "Elders, when I was young I found strange ruins in a hidden cove. Carvings on the stones glowed at my touch..."

The elders exchanged knowing looks. "Show us," the elder commanded.

In a hidden inlet, glowing runes covered ancient stones. The elder sang to them, and a portal opened with a flash. On the other side, a vast alien world stretched as far as the eye could see.

The elder turned to his pods. "Sarah may have found her way to this place, through means we do not comprehend. But wherever she is, she fights still for all people of the seas. We must have faith that when we are needed most, she will return."

And so the pods returned to their waters, keeping vigil and passing down the tale of Sarah's courage. Though her quest led to strange new lands, in spirit she remained with her pod forever. One day, when a new threat emerges, Sarah may come again to unite all people against the darkness. Her story is only beginning.

Unlikely Allies

When the light faded, Sarah found herself alone on an alien shore. Strange spires stretched endlessly above barren rocks.

She called out but heard no reply, not even the song of her pod-kin. Fear and loneliness gripped her heart. Had she been transported somewhere beyond all life?

Exhausted, Sarah collapsed and slept. When she awoke, strange lights moved in the dusk. Hissing voices sent her diving for cover behind spires.

Peering out, she froze in shock. Bipedal figures in gleaming armor prowled the rocks, wielding strange weapons that crackled with energy. Their skin was pale blue, eyes black as the night.

Aliens - but were they friend or foe? Sarah watched, hoping to learn their nature. But one soon noticed her hiding place and cried out.

She braced for attack, but the alien merely called in its sibilant tongue. Another approached and replied, gesturing to lower its weapon. Had they come in peace?

Slowly, Sarah emerged from hiding with paws raised. The aliens studied her curiously without hostility. A chance for understanding - if only they could communicate.

As the aliens cautiously approached, Sarah remained still, hoping to convey she meant no harm. The one who had first spotted her reached out a bluish hand slowly.

Sarah stared at the three fingers and allowed the alien to touch her fin. Its skin was cold but smooth. It spoke softly to its companion, then gestured toward the spires in the distance.

Cautiously, Sarah followed as the aliens led the way across the barren rocks. Along the way, she studied them closely, intrigued by their sleek armor and graceful yet powerful stride.

They soon arrived at a towering spire that glimmered in the dim light. As they approached, a shimmering forcefield lowered, admitting them inside.

Sarah gasped - advanced technology filled the spire. Panels glowed with alien script. Were these beings truly so different from herself and the pods?

The aliens spoke to each other, then one turned to Sarah. A device in its hands projected flickering shapes that almost seemed... communicative.

Had these strange creatures found a way for her to understand? Sarah focused on the shapes, sensing a chance to form an unlikely alliance in this strange new world.

The shapes the alien projected began to take on meaning as Sarah concentrated. She started to pick out simple images - rocks, water, pods.

Encouraged, the alien projected more complex ideas - the glowing object, the flash of light, her arrival on this shore alone and afraid. Sarah nodded in understanding, amazed at this rudimentary form of communication.

She took a stick and drew in the dirt, sketching pods swimming together and facing the squid beast. The aliens studied her drawings intently. One spoke to the others, then projected an image of its own people in their gleaming ships, with a question mark.

Sarah nodded eagerly, conveying that the pods had battled a similar threat. The aliens looked at each other in surprise, then one spoke at length while projecting more images of their advanced technologies and vast starships.

Sarah began to understand - these beings were explorers who had detected strange energy readings on this world. They had come seeking knowledge of the glowing object's origin.

She projected the pods battling Magnus and his creations, then her confrontation with the squid. The aliens listened raptly to her story in images and gestures. When she finished, they conferred excitedly, having pieced together the events.

It seemed a bond of trust was forming between the unlikely duo. And with the aliens' help, Sarah might find a way to return to her pod-kin with a new alliance.

The aliens' discussion grew animated as they pieced together Sarah's story. One turned to her with an excited gesture.

An image formed - Sarah and the pods, standing proudly alongside the tall aliens in their gleaming ships. She understood their meaning - an offer of alliance and assistance.

Overcome with joy, Sarah swam circles around them, chittering happily. Laughter echoed in the spire as the aliens grasped her elation. A breakthrough!

One alien spoke at length, then projected a diagram of their ship. Sarah saw it could travel between the stars through some wondrous means. They were offering her passage home!

Wasting no time, the aliens readied their ship. Sarah swam eagerly alongside as they strode across the barren landscape. A shimmering orb rose from the rocks, growing until it blocked out the sky.

Sarah gasped to see the vast starship suspended above. As she and the aliens embarked, flying towards the stars, hope swelled in her heart.

Her mission was far from over, but new allies stood at her side. And soon, she would reunite with her pod-kin and share the promise of this unexpected bond between distant peoples. Wherever her journey led, Sarah knew that together, nothing could stand against them.

Answers in the Ashes

The alien starship sped through the void, its advanced engines bending the laws of physics. Sarah gazed out portholes in awe, seeing wonders never dreamed by her pod-kin.

After days of travel, the ship dropped out of hyperspace near a barren world. Sarah sensed this was no chance destination - the aliens had brought her here for a reason.

As they disembarked, Sarah shuddered at the desolation before her. Blackened spires clawed a burned-out sky, ashes drifting on toxic winds. Yet amid the ruins, something glimmered with an all-too-familiar light.

The aliens had detected its signal and come seeking answers. Sarah followed them cautiously into the ruins, keeping alert for danger.

Suddenly a scream rent the air. Sarah raced toward the sound and found an alien fending off a pack of savage creatures, like living shadows given form.

She leapt without hesitation, raking the creatures with her magic blade. They fell back with inhuman wails, regarding her with new caution. The alien nodded gratefully.

Together they pushed onward, eventually finding the source of the light - another pulsing artifact, encased in a metal sphere. But what dark power lay behind these mysterious objects? And how were they connected to Magnus.

As Sarah and the alien studied the artifact, the shadow creatures attacked again in force. Their claws scraped against the metal sphere, seeking a way inside.

Sarah and her new ally stood back to back, holding the creatures at bay. But they were slowly being overwhelmed. Then Sarah noticed glows appearing in the ruins - more aliens coming to their aid.

With their combined efforts, the tide began to turn. The creatures fell one by one until at last only one remained. Weakened, it lunged at Sarah but she sidestepped and plunged her blade through its inky form.

It dissolved into nothingness. Sarah turned to see the aliens had gathered around the sphere, scanning it intently. One spoke urgently to the others while pointing at a readout.

It seemed they had discovered something crucial. Sarah swam over, and the alien projected an image - the sphere contained some kind of malevolent code, similar to the corruption that had possessed Magnus and his creations.

Another image showed this code spreading like a virus throughout the galaxy, warping worlds into dead husks. Sarah understood at last - the artifacts were no mere trinkets, but vessels for a cosmic plague.

The aliens had more questions than answers still. But one thing was clear - to save all peoples, living and yet to come, the source of this evil must be found and stopped.

As the aliens continued studying the artifact, Sarah gazed out at the desolate ruins. Something nagged at the edges of her mind, a half-remembered detail.

She swam quickly through the ashes, following a faint instinct. Soon she came upon a shattered dome, within an intact chamber. Etched on the metal walls were designs that made her breath catch.

Racing back to the others, Sarah grabbed a stick and drew furiously. The aliens watched, then gasped as her meaning became clear - the designs matched those left by Magnus in the corrupted forests.

This dead world had once harbored his like. Sarah showed images of Magnus, his machines, the possessed squid beast. A hush fell as the aliens grasped the connection.

One spoke gravely, projecting a new image - a vast cybernetic network, threads linking worlds across the cosmos. Magnus had been but one node in a sprawling infection, seeping through the stars.

Its source lay shrouded, manipulating species to further some inscrutable end. But these artifacts held clues to its nature, and perhaps vulnerabilities to exploit.

Sarah knew her mission now - to aid the aliens in unraveling this mystery, and bringing allies together from across the galaxy. Only by standing united could they face what lurked in the darkness pulling the strings.

Her journey was far from over, but hope had begun to kindle in the ashes of this ruined world.

With a new purpose and understanding, Sarah and the aliens worked tirelessly. Carefully extracting the artifact, they returned to the starship.

Back in orbit, scientists studied the mysterious code for weaknesses. Slowly patterns emerged - triggers that could short-circuit its corruptive influence. While its origins remained shrouded, chinks in its armor were revealed.

Communications were sent across known space, calling all species to arms against the spreading shadow. Messages of unity and hope, borne on the wings of allies new and old.

In time, replies came flooding in. Worlds once thought lost lit up again as infection was purged. Fleets assembled, bearing representatives of a hundred civilizations. And at the fore was a podling and her faithful alien friends.

Finally all was ready. Targeting the triggers uncovered, the great fleet activated powerful energy pulses. Across the galaxy, artifacts flared then dimmed as corruption dissolved.

In a dark region of unknown space, something screamed in fury. Its grip had been broken, its designs foiled. But its nature was still cloaked in the mists of time.

Sarah knew the threat was not ended, only driven back for now. But bonds of trust and purpose had been forged between species, and light had begun to push back the darkness. Her mission was complete - for now.

Where the shadows gathered again, she would be there to stand with her allies, old and new. This was only the beginning.

***

Chapter 09

LEARNING FROM THE LOCALS

Learning from the locals

After their victory over the spreading corruption, Sarah and her new allies took time to rest. The fleet dispersed to their homeworlds while deeper mysteries remained unsolved.

Sarah remained with the alien explorers, her bond with them strong. As their starship entered a remote region, long-range scans detected an inhabited world below showing no signs of infection.

"Perhaps here we will find locals willing to share their knowledge," said the elder alien Sarah had befriended. She nodded, hopeful new allies could be made.

They landed the ship on a grassy plain. Strange fluted calls echoed in the distance as bulbous trees swayed in breezes. Cautiously, Sarah and a squad of aliens disembarked.

The calls grew louder, then a herd of creatures emerged - hexapeds with iridescent hides and eye stalks swaying above. They slowed at seeing the newcomers, regarding them curiously without fear.

Sarah extended a fin in greeting, making soft chittering sounds. The creatures replied in musical tones, stalk eyes focusing on each alien in turn. They seemed peaceful and intelligent - would contact be possible?

As the elder alien activated its translation device, Sarah sensed an opportunity to learn from these beings and further the cause of galactic cooperation. Her mission of unity was far from over.

The elder alien spoke slowly into its device, and a soothing melodic voice emerged in reply from the herd's leader.

Though meanings were simple, communication had begun. The leader gestured its people forward, inviting the newcomers to follow across the plains. Sarah swam eagerly alongside, taking in colorful flowers and strange winged insects flitting between bulbous trees.

That evening, they arrived at the herd's settlement - domed structures woven from tall grasses, glowing softly within. More of the hexapeds emerged, unafraid, and a feast was laid out - fruits and tubers native to the world.

Sarah and the aliens joined the herd, communicating through images and gestures. The locals were called Althani, lived peacefully for generations on this world. Their songs told of observing the skies, but no contact until now.

After the meal, the elder Althani leader spoke at length, then showed images of the herd nurturing the land. Sarah projected the spreading corruption's defeat, conveying new allies were sought to prevent its return.

The Althani conferred softly, then their leader replied in song - their people would gladly share what knowledge they had amassed, in service of cooperation between all worlds. Sarah sensed a new bond was forming, furthering her mission's cause.

Over subsequent days, Sarah and the aliens learned much from the Althani. Through song, images and experience out on the plains, they studied the intricate balance the herd maintained with their environment.

The Althani showed how each plant and animal fulfilled a purpose, and how careful observation of the skies had taught them to predict subtle shifts in weather. Their mastery of this world was profound.

In turn, Sarah and the aliens shared tales of their own homes and the recent crisis. The Althani listened raptly, then their leader spoke a somber song - their records showed other worlds in this region fall silent long ago, perhaps victims of the same corruption.

This gave Sarah and her friends grave concern. If the threat had spread so far, was any place truly safe? They thanked the Althani for the warning, knowing it underscored how vital cooperation was to early detection.

Days passed swiftly as understanding grew between the groups. But Sarah sensed a restlessness in the aliens, eager to press on in their exploration. It was with heavy hearts they prepared to depart, having found true allies among the Althani.

At the edge of the plains, Sarah bid farewell to the herd's leaders. Through song and touch, they conveyed the bonds that would endure between their peoples even with distance. Unity was taking root throughout the stars.

As Sarah and the aliens' ship rose into the sky, she gazed back at the Althani herd one last time. Their melodic calls echoed a bittersweet farewell across the swaying grasslands.

Though her mission had succeeded in forging new bonds of cooperation, darker mysteries still lingered at the edge of knowledge. Sarah was determined to aid her allies in uncovering any further signs of the spreading corruption.

Together they would work to establish early warning networks and response plans, ensuring no threat could catch the growing galactic community off guard. With open communication and unity of purpose, their united fleets would be ready to face any resurgence.

And so Sarah's journey continued among the stars, as an ambassador of understanding between species. Wherever her travels led, she would carry the lessons learned from peaceful beings like the Althani - that through shared knowledge and mutual respect, even the most disparate of peoples could overcome past divisions.

Cooperation, not conflict, would light their path forward. And in time, the whole of creation might come to mirror the harmony she had found with her unlikely allies, old and new. Sarah's mission had only begun.

Wherever darkness gathered its forces once more, she would be there to stand with all those who chose the path of unity and peace. This was but one chapter in the eternal story.

A New Perspective

As their starship sailed the void, Sarah spent hours immersed in the aliens' vast database, soaking in perspectives from across the stars. But no records contained insights into her own mysterious pod-people.

One day, long-range sensors detected a class M planet with bipedal sentients living in scattered settlements. Sensing an opportunity, Sarah requested they investigate. The aliens obliged, curious about these ground-dwellers.

They landed stealthily near a walled village as the sun rose over jagged mountains. Peering out, Sarah glimpsed structures like nothing in her experience. But were these beings friendly? Only contact would reveal.

Taking a breath, she emerged from the ship with an alien escort. At first, the villagers stared in shock at the strange arrivals. But Sarah extended her fins in a gesture of peace, hoping to establish understanding as she had with so many others.

After long moments, a grizzled elder emerged and spoke cautiously in an unfamiliar tongue. The alien's translator processed and replied, as Sarah projected calm images through the device. A tentative communication had begun, opening a window to new perspectives.

As the elder listened to the alien's translated words and studied Sarah's projected images, a spark of curiosity kindled in his eyes. He called to the wary villagers, who began to murmur and gather closer.

The elder then gestured for Sarah and the aliens to follow. They walked with the villagers into the settlement, taking in strange sights - stone dwellings with thatched roofs, people in colorful woven garments, pens holding unfamiliar livestock.

The elder led them to a central gathering place and had them sit. Villagers looked on, uncertainty giving way to open interest. Children even approached Sarah tentatively, touching her slick skin with smiles.

Through images and translation, Sarah's group conveyed their peaceful mission of exploration and cooperation. The elder nodded slowly, then spoke at length while gesturing to the mountains and sky.

"He welcomes you as the first outsiders they've known," the alien translated. "This village has lived simply for generations, observing the heavens but unable to reach them. Your arrival is a sign that greater things may be possible."

Sarah sensed an opportunity to share knowledge that could help these people, and to learn about new perspectives in turn. Understanding was taking root between their disparate kinds.

Over the following days, lively exchanges took place between Sarah's group and the villagers. Through demonstration and shared meals, they conveyed insights into fields from medicine to engineering.

In return, the villagers taught of living in harmony with the rugged terrain, with lessons in herbalism, crafts and self-sufficient ways. Sarah was fascinated by their songs and stories passed down through oral tradition.

Most intriguing were the elders' tales of ancestors who once dwelled among the stars, but were lost to memory. Could this isolated village hold clues to some greater past? Sensing potential, Sarah requested to join one of their expeditions up the mountains.

After some discussion, the elders agreed. At dawn, Sarah set out with a party of villagers familiar with the treacherous slopes. Sure-footed, they guided her past jagged outcroppings and rushing streams toward a high glacier.

As they climbed, Sarah gained new respect for these people and their resilience. By midday they reached a hidden valley, and the elders' eyes lit up at ancient ruins half-buried in snow. Sarah scanned them eagerly, hoping for insights into the end of her own people. Had some mystery from the past been uncovered?

As Sarah helped the villagers uncover more of the mysterious ruins, she noticed strange markings and remnants of advanced alloys that did not match the village's simple technology. It seemed this isolated spot held secrets waiting to be revealed.

That evening, Sarah shared her findings with the alien scientists. They were intrigued and wished to study the site more closely. The village elders agreed, welcoming the opportunity for greater understanding.

In the weeks that followed, the combined efforts of villagers, aliens and Sarah brought more discoveries to light. Through carbon dating and material analysis, they learned this civilization had peake over a thousand years ago before descending into isolation.

While many questions remained, it was proof that even seemingly primitive peoples held remnants of greater pasts within their oral traditions. As the elders said, greater things were indeed possible if different kinds joined in cooperation.

With new friendships and knowledge gained, Sarah bid farewell to the villagers. But she vowed to return someday, and help them rediscover lost technologies to make life easier in their harsh homeland.

All who open themselves to diverse perspectives, she had learned, gain a richer view of the true tapestry of life. Her mission of fostering understanding between disparate peoples would continue across the stars.

The Stranger's Secret

As their starship sailed the void once more, Sarah pondered all that had been learned. Yet mysteries remained - chiefly about her own pod-people and their fate.

One night, sensors detected an escape pod drifting lifeless in a nearby system. The aliens towed it aboard for study, finding it decades old but intact. Within, they discovered a lone survivor - a strange, octopus-like being clinging to life.

Sarah and the medics worked swiftly, reviving the stranger with fluids and warmth. As consciousness returned, large eyes blinked in confusion at the aliens surrounding it. Sensing its fear, Sarah moved between to project calm through touch.

A flurry of clicks and chirps followed as the stranger regained strength. The aliens' translator analyzed and replied, as Sarah showed welcoming images of cooperation between species. Slowly, understanding took shape.

The stranger came from a world called Orth, where its people had dwelled for eons. But some cataclysmic event had rendered the planet uninhabitable, forcing mass evacuation. In the chaos, this pod had been jettisoned by accident into the depths of space.

Sarah sensed an opportunity to gain new insight through this castaway. If she could but earn its trust, secrets long buried might come to light.

As the stranger recovered, Sarah ensured it was treated with compassion. In turn, it began sharing more of its people and homeworld.

The Orthians lived harmoniously with the oceans, but strange seismic shifts rocked their islands years ago. Volcanic eruptions darkened the skies, choking waters with ash. Evacuation vessels were launched, but this pod had malfunctioned during launch.

Alone in the void, its life support slowly failed until the aliens' chance discovery. Sarah sensed this matched descriptions of her own pod-people, cast adrift in similar mysterious circumstances.

Through images, she conveyed her quest for understanding her origins. The stranger regarded her with new interest, then projected memories of archives containing ancient texts. Records that predated even the Orthians' earliest history spoke of beings like Sarah, scattered to the stars when a great cataclysm destroyed their world.

Hope surged within her! At last, clues were emerging. She requested the aliens help the stranger recover, hoping in time it might guide them to the archives' location. Understanding the past could help safeguard the future.

As the stranger recovered its strength, bonds of trust grew between it and Sarah. Each day it shared more of its people and culture, fascinated by her quest for origins.

Weeks passed before the Orthian was strong enough to guide the ship. Under star charts it projected, the aliens' navigators plotted a course to a remote system. There, orbiting a blue giant star, was a small rocky world that scans showed breathable atop ancient stone spires.

The archives. Sarah swam eagerly beside the viewports as they approached. Crumbling temples and statues were visible, bearing familiar swirling symbols. This place held untold secrets from before recorded history.

They landed amid the ruins under bright skies. As Sarah and the Orthian disembarked, feelings welled within unlike anything before. Ancestral memory stirred at every crumbling wall and glyph-marked pillar.

Guided by its memories, the Orthian led them into the largest temple's depths. There, in a hidden chamber, were shelves of aged tablets bearing the swirling script. Sarah ran her digits across the markings, understanding dawning in her mind. At last, answers were within reach.

The Orthian projected its memories of how to access the archives' ancient database. Under flickering lights, holograms and translations appeared showing histories far predating any known species.

Sarah learned of a lush water world, home to her pod-people for eons before a cosmic catastrophe struck without warning. Massive earthquakes and volcanic eruptions rendered the planet uninhabitable, forcing a desperate evacuation.

Many escape vessels were launched carrying cryogenically preserved colonists like herself, intended to reseed the galaxy if the homeland could not be restored.

But something had gone wrong - systems failures, collisions in space, and the pods were scattered alone across the stars with no means of waking their sleeping passengers.

Until now. At last, Sarah understood her origins among a people long lost. But she took solace knowing their legacy of exploration lived on through her and the bonds she had forged. No longer adrift, she had found purpose guiding a new era of cooperation.

Sarah thanked the Orthian, having helped illuminate dark chapters of the past. Together with her new friends old and new, the future looked bright. Her mission would continue across the stars, ensuring all peoples had a place to call home and were never alone.

Changing Course

With new insights gained, Sarah felt her mission shifting focus. No longer was she simply exploring - she now understood her role protecting remnants of lost peoples like herself.

As their starship sailed the stars once more, Sarah shared her revelations with the aliens. They were intrigued yet concerned, sensing her desire to seek out other scattered pods. But such a quest could take lifetimes, and what of the growing threats they had vowed to monitor?

That night, Sarah gazed pensively at the swirling nebulae outside. Part of her yearned to reunite with any kin who still slept, unaware of the galaxy changing around them. But lives beyond her own depended on the watchfulness of allies like these.

She was pulled from thought by the aliens' captain, bearing grave news - sensors had detected signs of the mysterious corruption spreading to a strategically vital system. If allowed to take hold, countless worlds could be imperiled. They agreed the situation demanded investigation.

As the ship changed course, Sarah sensed a shifting of priorities. Her mission of understanding different lifeforms now merged with protecting the diversity she had come to cherish. Where danger gathered its forces, there she and her friends would stand united.

The starship raced toward the troubled system. En route, Sarah met with the captain and scientists to plan their response.

Analysis of sensor readings showed the corruption spreading via anomalous space-time distortions, somehow warping minds and wills. Its origins remained unclear. They agreed stealth and caution were paramount to avoid confrontation until the threat was better understood.

Arriving, they cloaked the ship and sent probes for close analysis. To their horror, entire planets showed signs of the population falling under some insidious control. Communications were dominated by paranoid rhetoric, as citizens turned against off-worlders and each other.

If this chaos spread, it could destabilize the region. They needed to infiltrate the core worlds and find the source. But first, they scanned for any free or resistant individuals to contact. Perhaps understanding local conditions could offer clues.

Just then, a distress call pierced the comms - a small ship fleeing orbital bombardment. Its pilot was wounded but coherent, begging aid for her resistance cell. An opportunity had emerged, but also grave risk.

The starship raced to intercept the damaged vessel. Bringing it aboard, they found the pilot gravely injured but stabilized her with medical nanites.

As she regained consciousness, Sarah was at her side. "Be at peace, we mean only to help. What has happened here?"

The pilot, named Sila, eyed them warily. "Our worlds have fallen under some...influence. It twists minds and sparks violence. My cell was exposed trying to understand it."

She explained how societal divisions had erupted overnight as the corruption spread. Only a few retained clear thoughts while neighbors turned on each other in paranoid frenzies.

"This influence—can you describe its nature? We've detected similar events and want to understand its source," Sarah said gently.

Sila shook her head. "It defies explanation. A shadow passing through the mind... I only hope others in my cell survived." She pleaded for their help making contact.

Sarah assured her, "Rest now. We'll do what we can to aid your people while seeking answers. Together perhaps we can overcome this threat."

With Sila stabilized, Sarah met with the aliens to plan their next move. They agreed attempting direct contact with infected populations carried too much risk. Instead, Sarah would accompany

Sila back under cloak to rendezvous with any surviving resistance, while the ship conducted long-range scans for anomalies.

As Sila healed, she bonded with Sarah, impressed by her drive to understand others. In turn, Sarah learned more about the vibrant cultures now imperiled. It steeled her resolve to uncover the source of the corruption and prevent more needless suffering.

When the time came, Sila guided them to a remote safehouse in ruinous mountains. To their relief, several others had also escaped the violence. Introductions were made, and after some discussion, the group agreed to work with their new allies.

With the resistance's local knowledge and Sarah's insights from afar, they began strategizing how to stay one step ahead of the influence while searching for answers. Its reach seemed to spread through subtle manipulation of fears and divisions, but to what end? Together, they were determined to thwart its schemes and set the people free once more.

***

Chapter 10

CALMER WATERS

Calmer Waters

After weeks of stealth operations, Sarah's group had gathered troubling clues about the mysterious influence's spread and effects. But tracking its source proved elusive as it worked its corruption from the shadows.

One night, Sarah stood gazing at stars alongside Sila, who had become a close friend. "This influence is cunning, but we're learning from each encounter. Together I believe we can overcome it."

Sila nodded wearily. "Your optimism gives us strength. But this shadow knows our worlds and peoples well, using our flaws against us. I fear if it isn't stopped, nothing will remain of the civilization my ancestors built."

Sarah sensed her friend's mounting stress. "Come, let's take a transport and find calmer waters. A chance to breathe may offer new clarity."

Sila agreed, and they embarked under cloak. Sarah guided them to a remote green moon's sparkling seas, empty of settlements. As Sila gazed in wonder at the alien shoreline, Sarah said "This place is yours. Find respite that you may return refreshed."

Sila smiled gratefully at Sarah. As the moons's two suns sank towards the horizon, painting the sky in vibrant hues, she walked along the shoreline deep in thought.

The lapping of gentle waves soothed her frayed nerves. All around was a natural beauty untouched by conflict or corruption. She found a grassy bluff overlooking the sea and sat watching seabirds dance upon the wind.

Her mind slowly cleared of worries, instead filling with memories of carefree days from her youth. Back when her world knew only peace, and people found unity in their shared love of exploration and discovery.

She sensed Sarah's kindness in bringing her to this place. For the first time in weeks, hope began to kindle again within her heart. As long as there were those willing to stand together against darkness, it could be overcome.

By the time Sarah joined her at sunset, a calm resolve had taken hold. She smiled at her friend. "Thank you for this respite. The shadows seem less ominous having seen places of light still remain. Let's return renewed in purpose - to ensure the preservation of beauty in all its forms."

As night fell, the two friends sat gazing at the moon's twin stars sparkling on the water.

"Your words give me hope," Sarah said. "In all my travels, I've found light still shines where people come together in compassion. Our differences pale before what we share."

Sila nodded. "That is the truth the influence hopes we forget. But together with allies like you, we can remember our shared hopes and protect each other's freedoms." She sighed. "Though this threat is cunning, hitting where it hurts most."

"It preys on fear and division," Sarah agreed. "We must stand as a beacon of unity. And where it has corrupted, bring understanding to open minds once more."

Renewed in spirit, they returned to their camp. There, Sila addressed her people with newfound resolve. Though dark times lay ahead, together with friends old and new, they would overcome this shadow threatening to extinguish their world's light.

Heartened, the resistance pledged to redouble efforts understanding the influence and protecting communities from its reach. Where it brought fear, they would sow hope. And one day, they were determined to uncover its source and end its schemes for good.

he following day, Sila and Sarah met with the resistance leaders to plan their next moves. Using insights gained from their time on the moon, they developed a multi-pronged strategy.

Scouting parties would infiltrate infected regions to monitor the influence's spread and counter its propaganda with messages of unity. Medics would seek out isolated communities to bolster defenses against mental manipulation. And technicians worked to enhance sensors, hoping to detect any anomalies that may reveal the origin of the corruption.

Meanwhile, Sarah returned to her ship to share all that was learned. The aliens aided the analysis, discovering the influence seemed to generate subtle gravitational and electromagnetic fields to subtly alter brain function on a mass scale. This provided new clues to pursue.

Heartened by witnessing the resilience of Sila's people, Sarah was more committed than ever to this alliance. Through open-minded cooperation and compassion for all, she believed any threat could be overcome. And one day, lost peoples like herself may find safe harbor once more among the stars.

With renewed hope, the resistance and their allies prepared for the challenges ahead. Working as one, they were determined to thwart the influence's schemes, and bring light back to the worlds now shrouded in shadow.

Understanding Found

Weeks passed as the alliance's multi-pronged efforts took effect. Sila's scouts monitored the influence's movements while medics strengthened remote communities.

Meanwhile, analyses from Sarah's ship detected strange energy fluctuations from a remote star system. Could this be the origin they sought? They plotted an intercept course.

Arriving, scans found two planets harboring advanced civilizations, yet both populations had fallen under complete control. Strange spires dotted the surfaces, resonating with the same anomalous energies.

Cautiously, Sarah and Sila led an away mission to the larger world's surface. All seemed eerily serene as they approached an empty city. "Stay alert, this calm likely masks the influence's true nature," warned Sarah.

Suddenly, strange figures appeared - the locals, but moved with inhuman poise and glowing eyes. "We mean no harm, only to understand," Sarah spoke calmly.

The figures replied as one: "All will be understood in time. Resistance is futile, assimilation inevitable." Their words held a subtle, hypnotic edge.

The alliance members resisted an urge to comply. Had they found the influence's source? And could its control be overcome?

As the figures advanced, Sila noticed movement in the city behind them. "Sarah, look!" she whispered.

Through windows, they saw normal citizens going about lives. But some moved as if in a trance, others fought an invisible struggle.

Sarah called to the figures, "We see your control is not absolute. There is hope to be free!"

Her words seemed to trigger something. The figures shuddered, eyes flickering. "Control... fading. Must... recalibrate."

Sensing an opportunity, Sila said, "Fight it! You have a will of your own."

The figures trembled violently. One cried, "So... long under its sway. Help... us!"

Sarah nodded. "Tell us how to shut off its signal without harming your people. Together we'll end its reign."

After a moment of static, the figure spoke weakly but clearly. "The... spires. Destroy... central spire to sever... control matrix."

It gave coordinates before the glow faded from its eyes. The figures collapsed, now dormant.

Sarah smiled at Sila. "Progress! Let's free this world, then seek the source of the influence's power."

The group made their way across the eerily empty city to the tallest spire at its center. Upon scanning it, they discovered it was emitting powerful electromagnetic pulses that seemed to be manipulating the minds of the populace.

"We need to disable it without causing damage," said Sarah. After some analysis of its structure, one of the resistance engineers believed she had found a way. "If I can reroute the power flow through this conduit, it should safely shut down the signal."

Carefully she went to work, bypassing circuits and rerouting cables with practiced precision. The others kept watch nervously. After some tense minutes, the pulsing from the spire began to slow and weaken.

As the last flicker died away, an echoing cheer arose across the city. People had begun emerging from buildings, rubbing their heads in confusion. The glow left their eyes, replaced by awareness.

One man approached the group tentatively. "You...freed us? We've been in some kind of daze." Sarah reassured him with a smile. "The influence is gone. You're in control of your world once more."

Elated, the man introduced himself as the city's leader. "Thank you! But this malevolent force still endangers others. Please, let us aid your mission to stop it at its source."

With the people of that world freed from the influence's control, a sense of hope and determination filled the air.

Sarah and Sila were overjoyed at this major victory and new alliance. With the locals' help, they began planning their assault on the central spire emitting the controlling signals across the whole system.

As engineers worked to modify the starship to withstand the spire's defenses, Sila took the time to bond with the newly liberated citizens. She was moved by their resilience in throwing off the influence's yoke. It reinforced her belief that wherever free will and compassion existed, darkness could not prevail.

At last, the day came to launch the mission. With the city leader and a squadron of freed citizens at their side, Sarah and Sila boarded the starship. This may be the final confrontation to break the influence's insidious grip for good. As the spire loomed ahead, a sense of destiny filled them all. They were determined to see this shadowy menace banished and allow the light of these peoples to shine freely once more across the stars.

A Protector's Role

The starship raced towards the spire emitting the controlling signals. Sensors detected powerful energy shields and weapons awaiting them.

"Stay strong, we can overcome this," said Sarah to Sila and the others. She addressed the ship. "Divert all power to forward shields and armaments. Prepare to break through on my signal."

As the spire's defenses engaged, pounding their shields, Sarah shouted "Now!" Volleys of precision fire struck key points, overloading shields in flashes of light.

Seeing an opening, Sarah dove the ship inside. They emerged in a vast chamber housing the spire's heart - a pulsing orb suspended by energy beams.

Figures appeared and attacked, but the newly freed citizens fought back fiercely to defend their protectors. Sila faced one and said "You don't have to do this. Fight the control!"

Its eyes flickered. "Must...obey. It is our...purpose." Sila pleaded, "Every being deserves freedom. Let me help you break its hold!"

Slowly, the figure faltered as Sila's words awakened its dormant will. It cried out and collapsed. She embraced it compassionately. "You've taken the first step. Stay strong - your people need you."

As the battle raged, Sila helped more throw off their mental shackles. Soon the tide turned as the figures began aiding the alliance instead of attacking.

With the locals' help, Sarah analyzed the pulsing orb's structure. "There, a centralized control node. Disable it and the whole system should shut down."

The ship's weapons charged for a precision strike. But suddenly, the orb flickered and from it emerged a vast, shadowy presence. tendrils snaked towards the ship with a psychic force that overwhelmed shields.

It's...fighting back directly now!" cried Sarah. The entity boomed in their minds "You cannot stop what is inevitable. All will join or be destroyed."

Sila replied calmly "You force control through fear. But together, free peoples are stronger than any single power." The entity wavered, not used to resistance.

Sarah had an idea. "Divert all power to communications! Sila, help me broadcast a message of hope and unity across the system!"

As the entity bore down, their combined voices rang out: "Citizens of the stars, your protector seeks only freedom for all. Stand with us against the darkness!"

As Sarah and Sila's message echoed across the system, people began to stir from their mental haze. On countless worlds, they shook off the influence and realized they were not alone.

A swelling chorus of voices joined the transmission, each one adding their strength. "We will not live as slaves any longer!" "The light of freedom guides us!" "All beings deserve to choose their own path!"

The entity reeled under the onslaught of unified free will. Its tendrils retracted from the ship as it lost coherence. Sila smiled, "You see? Together we are more than a match for any shadow."

Sarah targeted the control node. "Now! For the freedom of all peoples!" Their combined fire struck true, obliterating the node in a flash.

The entity shrieked and dissolved into nothing as its machinery shut down. Across the system, spires crumbled into dust. The people had won.

Wild cheers broke out on every world. Sila embraced Sarah, overcome with joy at what they had achieved. "A new era begins today. All will know that as long as there are those willing to stand as one, no darkness can overcome the light of freedom."

In the aftermath, the people worked to rebuild after casting off the influence's yoke. With the alliance's help, cooperation and understanding flourished between species once more.

Word of the victory spread fast. Delegations from systems long cut off by the shadows arrived daily, eager to reconnect. Sarah was heartened to see old alliances renewed.

As for Sila's people, they began assisting others still plagued by remnants of the influence. Together with their new friends, no trace of the darkness would be left behind.

In time, a grand celebration was held across many worlds. Sarah and Sila stood before the crowds, who cheered not just for their role but for each other - proof that united, even the greatest threats could be overcome.

Looking to the stars, Sila said to Sarah "Our work is just beginning. But as long as there are protectors willing to stand for all peoples' freedoms, the light of hope will never fade from the galaxy."

Sarah smiled, taking her hand. "And you will always have an ally by your side, my friend. Our mission continues - to ensure all may journey together in peace beneath the stars."

New Beginnings

Years passed as Sarah and Sila's alliance worked to mend wounds left by the influence across many worlds. Cooperation and trust were slowly rebuilt.

One day, Sarah received a transmission from her people. "We've made breakthroughs understanding the influence. Its power came from exploiting mental vulnerabilities in developing societies. Come, there is more to discuss."

Sarah shared the news with Sila, who had become like family. "This could provide insight to prevent recurrence. Will you join me in returning to my people?"

Sila smiled. "Of course. Our mission is not over, and I wish to know more of the aliens who count me as friend. Let us go together."

They boarded Sarah's ship and embarked. Upon arrival, Sarah was overjoyed to reunite with her people. Sila also warmly greeted the aliens, impressed by their advances.

At a gathering, the aliens' leader spoke: "Our studies show with care and guidance, younger species can fortify their minds and societies to withstand such manipulation."

Sarah nodded. "This knowledge must be shared. No one should face such threats alone again." She turned to Sila. "What do you think - shall we spread the word throughout the stars?"

Sila smiled at Sarah. "Nothing would make me prouder than to continue our work helping others. With this new understanding, we can forge a future where all peoples grow in freedom and friendship."

The aliens' leader spoke again. "To that end, we offer our most advanced starship to serve as your vessel. With its power and technologies, you will be well equipped to aid any in need across the galaxy."

Sarah and Sila embraced joyfully. A new chapter was unfolding! They boarded the magnificent starship, awe-struck by its capabilities.

As they embarked on their first mission, Sila gazed out at the stars. So much had changed since that fateful day they first met in battle. "Who could have imagined where our path would lead? Now we have the means to ensure no one faces darkness alone."

Sarah agreed. "And it seems our alliance was but the first step towards a new era of cooperation throughout the cosmos. As long as there are those willing to stand as protectors, the light of hope and freedom will keep spreading further into the galaxy."

Their first mission took them to a developing world struggling with internal conflicts that outside forces threatened to exploit. Upon arriving, Sarah and Sila met with leaders from the various factions.

"We are not here to take sides, but offer aid so you can resolve differences peacefully," said Sarah. Sila added, "Unity is your strongest shield against those who would sow division."

The leaders were skeptical at first. But Sarah and Sila shared what they had learned - how supporting each other's well-being and giving all peoples a voice leads to stronger, more resilient societies.

After much discussion, one leader said "You speak wisdom. Our squabbles pale before threats that could enslave us all." Another agreed, "Together as equals, perhaps we can build the future we all want."

Hope bloomed as cooperation slowly replaced old grudges. Sarah and Sila helped mediate, finding common ground and fair compromises. In time, a new constitution was drafted guaranteeing all peoples a stake in their world's destiny.

At the signing, Sarah said "This marks a new dawn. May your unity and goodwill spread throughout the stars as an example." Cheers rose as new bonds of fellowship were forged. The people had taken the first step towards a brighter tomorrow.

With their first success under their belts, Sarah and Sila continued their mission of helping worlds build resistance to darkness through unity and empowerment.

Over the years, many more systems were aided as threats to free peoples everywhere diminished. Word of the protectors' good works spread widely, becoming a symbol of hope.

As the alliance celebrated decades of progress, a grand ceremony was held. Representatives from across the protected worlds gathered to express gratitude. But it was Sila who best summed up what had been achieved:

"When Sarah and I first met in battle, we were strangers on opposite sides. But our willingness to understand one another led us to realize we all seek the same things - freedom, justice, community. And so we vowed to help any in need, so that no one would have to face oppression alone ever again."

"Today, that dream has been realized across the stars. Old divisions have fallen away as we recognize our shared hopes. Darkness will always lurk, but as long as protectors stand united with all peoples, our light of fellowship will endure."

Amid the applause, Sarah took Sila's hand and smiled proudly. Though their work was never done, in that moment they took heart - for they had helped shape a legacy of cooperation that would outlast even the farthest-reaching stars.

***

Summary

The story is set in a small coastal fishing village that relies on the bounty of the sea. Sarah lives alone near the edge of the village and helps the elderly fisherman Thomas with his catch. One morning, Sarah and Thomas witness a strange glowing object crash into the ocean with an explosion. An eerie pulsating glow emerges underwater. Another larger impact unleashes a shrieking sea monster.

More objects continue falling, each crash worse than the last. Strange glowing creatures emerge from the depths, displaying unknown powers. Sarah sees a gigantic flaming creature give violent birth on the shore. The creatures spread unknown plagues killing local wildlife. Fish and seabirds wash up dead with gruesome lesions. Tide pools become choked with diseased crabs and deceased marine life.

As the creatures grow aggressive, Sarah and Thomas narrowly escape while surveying the depths. They flee to the cliffs as the monsters pursue with shocking speed. Trapped by the tide, they fight off giant beasts attempting to scale the rocks. The community realizes they face a war for survival. Strange mists and glows appear as scouts report more shapes in the waters. Under Father Michael, the villagers fortify homes against the sea menace.

Though prevailing in their first clash, larger creatures still emerge. The monsters display coordination, battling over territory. Further hit-and-run assaults mount along the coast and cliffs. A greater force emerges to hunt the villagers. Strange lights move inland at night with chilling howls. Scouts disappear near eerie mists. An immense shadow approaches the village under fading light.

The creatures drive becomes to eliminate all humans interfering in their domain. Assaults grow bolder, unwilling to rest until the villagers are dead or driven away. Supplies dwindle against the alien foes. Sarah volunteers to lead a scouting party into the accursed waters and hills, hoping to learn weaknesses. Though risky, others join to no longer stand idle.

In gathering gloom, Sarah's band sets out towards the mists and glows, to either win back their land or perish in the attempt. What secrets they may discover in the monsters' domain remains unseen. But this act of bravery offers their only chance to turn the tide.

The novel depicts the villagers' desperate struggle against escalating alien terrors that emerge to threaten their isolated way of life. Sarah risks all to discover what may decide the fate of the besieged fishing village.

About the Author

Mustafa A. Nejem is a maritime visionary with a captain's heart and an island soul. In his island home, the sea's love, sailing's legacy, and leadership's flame passed down through generations with pride and glory. He is a skilled navigator of words, charting a course through the vast ocean of knowledge. With his expertise and passion , he guide readers towards prosperous shores, unveiling the secrets of maritime life and business success in concise and captivating prose.

www.ingramcontent.com/pod-product-compliance
Lightning Source LLC
Chambersburg PA
CBHW080851120626
46546CB00008B/2777